HERB MAGIC
Garden *and* Craft

HERB MAGIC
and Garden Craft

By *Louise Evans Doole*

STERLING
PUBLISHING CO., Inc.   New York

Oak Tree Press Co., Ltd.
London & Sydney

OTHER BOOKS OF INTEREST

Exotic Mushrooms
Gardening with Herbs for Flavor and Fragrance
How to Enjoy Your Weeds

ISBN 0-8069-3920-6   UK 7061 2395-6
3921-4

Contents

PART III GARDEN CRAFTING

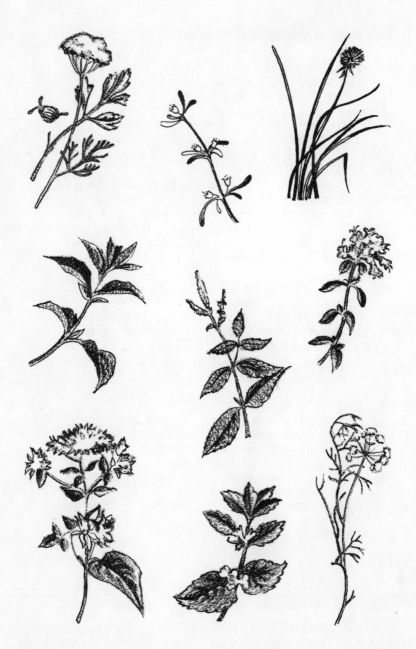

Part I.
HOW TO GROW HERBS

1. Plant Herbs for Happiness

This is not a book for professionals. It is for those who would like to grow a few herbs for fun, fragrance and flavor. If you find excitement in doing things with an extra fillip, if you like watching things grow, and want to add spice to your life, there is no better way than with herbs.

Herbs are known to have been used as far back as 3000 B.C. Helen of Troy was gathering elecampane root when Paris carried her away, and in 812 A.D. Charlemagne compiled a list of 75 herbs to be planted on his grounds. Of these, perhaps 18 are still in use in our own gardens.

In 1573 Tusser, a retainer in the court of James I of England, published "500 Points of Good Husbandry," a rhyming gardening book. He listed as essential seven types of herbs, including:

21 kinds of strewing herbs
42 seeds and herbs for the kitchen
22 herbs and roots for salads and sauces
40 herbs, branches and flowers for windows and pots
28 herbs necessary to grow in the garden for physic
Herbs and roots to boil or to butter

Many of the herbs he named are now unknown, and certainly most of them are unnecessary for the person growing herbs for pleasure.

Through the centuries, the herb garden lost much of its importance. But in colonial days in the United States, nearly every housewife had her "simples" growing in the "yarb" patch. Today herbs have come into their own as condiments and pot herbs as well as for their fragrance. Many of the ones we use are the same as those which Charlemagne brought into his gardens.

Herbs are great reputation-makers—and savers. I remember a Sunday evening when out-of-town friends dropped in, and rashly I invited them to stay for supper. Only after they accepted did I remember that we had not eaten at home for several days; my cupboard was practically bare.

However, my husband, who truly has a "green thumb," brought in some prize tomatoes from the garden—both the large, deep gold and the rose-red, meaty beefsteak varieties. I arranged these in alternate thick slices. Then quick—to the herb patch! I snipped chives and scattered them on the red tomatoes, basil on the yellow. Then I put on a few sprigs of tender marjoram to decorate the whole. A plate of sandwiches, iced tea with fresh mint and lemon balm, warm brownies made from a packaged mix—and such rave notices! That was years ago, but our friends still compliment me on that simple meal!

There was another time when herbs saved my reputation as a hostess. We had invited a young couple to dinner. It was a hot day; I was exceptionally busy, and I am ashamed to say that I had been a bit careless about planning the meal.

To my surprise, the boy turned to his bride and said, "See? What did I tell you? I *said* that there would be something different!"

"Oh, but Bob!" I objected. "There really isn't anything

unusual at all." I wished desperately that I had given the meal a little more thought.

"There is, too!" he said triumphantly, and pointed to a row of pretty glasses marching down the center of the table. Each glass contained sprays of different herbs to be added to the iced tea: lemon mint, peppermint, spearmint, burnet and borage flowers. Since within our own family, opinions as to mint in tea vary greatly, I always serve it separately. I took it for granted that others did the same thing, but our guests thought my arrangement of mints glamorous and unusual!

At an informal dinner party I once used sprigs of half a dozen different kinds of herbs to garnish salad plates instead of lettuce. The guests had fun tasting each and trying to identify it. You'll be surprised how very few herbs most people can name.

There is another reason that growing herbs is a wonderful hobby—it can be a family project from planning the garden to drying the harvest. Let the children help. For centuries herbs have been mentioned in fairy tales and folklore, as well as in the Bible. Remember sesame from the story Ali Baba, the mustard seed of the Bible, or dittany mentioned in Virgil's *Aeneid?* Your children will love raising some of the herbs they have read about.

Since you don't have to be fussy about planting the seeds, a child can sprinkle them in the prepared bed. If the small seeds are mixed with sand, he will be less likely to get too many in one place. Later, he will take special delight in watching the different herbs grow; they will appeal to his senses of sight, smell and taste. The varied shapes of the leaves, the kitten-fuzz of applemint, the prickly feel of borage, the wonderful fragrances of mint, thyme and basil, the piquant taste when leaves are nibbled—all these will delight your children.

When they help you harvest, they will take pride in the

herbs which they have grown. Even a toddler can pick leaves and drop them into a jar for vinegar-making, or put bits of rose geranium or lemon verbena into jelly glasses for mother to fill with boiling liquid.

But before you think about harvesting, you will have to decide which herbs to plant. You may be astonished to realize how many herbs you are already growing. Parsley, chives, garlic, spearmint, dill and sage appear in almost every garden. And they are among the most valued herbs. Do you raise violets, roses, nasturtiums and marigolds? These, too, are herbs, even though we call them flowers.

Along with these herbs, add thyme, summer savory, sweet marjoram, basil, lemon balm (Melissa), borage and chervil, and you will have a good start on a herb garden which will provide for most of your needs.

Herbs are fun to grow, and they are easy to raise unless you choose to make a major project of it. Unfortunately, I have never developed a "green thumb"; most plants don't "just grow" for me. But herbs do. With very poor conditions, I manage to have all the herbs I want for myself or to give to friends.

Although herbs are supposed to need plenty of sunlight and an alkaline soil, mine get shade and clay. They do best with lots of space in which to grow; I have practically none. Our climate is dry, the winds hot, the growing season short. And still, should you stop by some afternoon, I can give you a cup of tea flavored with lemon balm, herb-flavored canapes, and buttered scones spread with rose geranium jelly.

Fortunately for lazy gardeners like myself, those herbs most frequently used are also the easiest grown. One packet of seeds for each will be more than enough. If you have only a small space, divide the seeds with a friend, or save some for a second planting later in the summer, for plants to take indoors during the winter.

When deciding which herbs to put in your garden, remember

that it must be suited to your particular way of life. If you enjoy entertaining and love to cook, you will want a garden planted mostly with culinary herbs. If you wish for fragrance primarily, you would choose some other herbs. Or if a collection of as many herbs as possible is your goal, still another plan would be needed.

Basic Herbs

Practically everyone who grows herbs has her own basic list, and you will not be long in finding yours. However, to start with, try these:

Sow seeds of:

Sweet basil	Parsley
Borage	Dill
Burnet	Sweet marjoram
Chervil	Summer savory

Get roots of:

Spearmint	Lemon balm
Peppermint	Chives (bulblets)

Get plants of:

Sage	Thyme
Rosemary	Lavender

The Culinary Seeds

Although when we speak of using herbs, we generally refer to the leaves, there are some which are better known for their seeds. Of these the most popular are:

Anise	Coriander	Mustard
Caraway	Cumin	Poppy
Cardamon	Dill	Sesame
Celery	Fennel	

Since the leaves as well as the seeds of fennel, mustard, dill, anise and caraway are used in cooking you may want to include one or all of them in your herb garden. However, herbs grown for their seed alone are scarcely worth the space and bother. The crop is too small to be of value, and you can buy fresh seed inexpensively packaged at any grocery store.

Ten Perennials to Buy

To start with, you will have to buy some plants. After they are well established, you can propagate your own as described in Chapter 5. Some will spread by themselves.

Chives are a "must" by the kitchen door. Your clump of chives will send up green spikes even before the snow is gone. The purple heads of their flowers are pretty among the long green leaves. Chop the leaves into anything which will take an onion taste.

Hyssop makes a good small hedge. It may be used sparingly in stews.

Lemon Balm spreads so rapidly and grows so fast that you will find it escaping to far parts of the garden. Its strong lemon flavor is good in iced drinks and hot tea, and it is a fragrant addition to sachets and potpourris.

Lovage grows to more than 6 feet tall. It is especially good in soups and makes a nice background plant.

Mint, whether it be spearmint, peppermint or applemint (sometimes called wooly mint), is easy to start from a root or cutting, but it must be confined, or it will pop up in every corner of the garden.

Rosemary is an evergreen. Plants are difficult to obtain, but if you can buy one about a foot high it will grow to 4 feet. You must take it indoors for the winter.

Sage, that well-known seasoning of poultry dressings, makes a pretty grey-green plant in a corner of the garden. I can never resist hanging a few sprays in the kitchen. It is nice both to smell and to look at.

Summer Savory is better than *Winter Savory* as a culinary herb. Since it is delicate, it may be safest to pot a plant or two for the indoor garden, unless you live in a part of the country where the winters are mild. The savories are especially good with fish and green beans.

Sweet Cicely is a giant chervil. This decorative plant has graceful, fernlike leaves and white flowers. The whole plant —leaves, roots and seeds—is anise-flavored.

Tarragon is best known for its use in vinegar and also gives a flavorsome accent to chicken and fish. Tarragon is a good herb to know about, but don't bother too much about having it in your garden. You can buy a bottle of tarragon vinegar much more easily than you can locate a plant.

Thyme is hardy, but it will do no harm to give it a thin covering of leaves for the winter. *Thyme vulgaris* is the one which you will want for cooking.

Ground Covers

There are several herbs which make good ground covers. *Thyme serphyllum* is one. Other old-fashioned herbs, well known to gardeners of Colonial days, are camomile (English), sweet woodruff and germander. Sweet woodruff will grow in the shade, but the others, including thyme, prefer sun.

Although the dried herbs which you can buy are good, their flavor cannot compete with your fresh-from-the-garden seasonings. Once you have plucked a fresh leaf of basil and dropped it in the stewed tomatoes, or smelled the tang of thyme as your foot brushes it on the garden path, you will never again be without your own garden of herbs.

The next chapter lists and describes many different varieties of herbs for you to choose from.

2. A Descriptive List of Herbs

These are the herbs which you are most likely to plant or about which you might like to know. Although there are usually several varieties of each, this list includes only those most commonly grown in our gardens. These herbs may all be grown outdoors, and those marked (I) may also be grown indoors. Naturally you will not grow them all, but this should help you make your choice.

ANGELICA (*Angelica atropurpurea*)

This American variety of angelica should be better known than it is. It is a striking background plant, growing as high as 6 to 8 feet. The large leaves resemble those of the tuberous begonia. Angelica has umbrels (umbrella-shaped whirls) of tiny white flowers. The entire plant—hollow stems, roots, seeds and young leaves—can be used. The stems are good candied, or blanched and eaten like celery or stewed with sugar as is fruit. The young leaves are delicious with fish.

Start self-sowing angelica from seed or plants, and let it grow either in a shady spot or in one which is at least partially shaded.

(I) ANISE (*Pimpinella anisum*)

This annual is grown mostly for its sweet, licorice-flavored seed. Its grey-green foliage is lacy and deeply notched. It has umbrels of tiny whitish flowers. Fresh leaves are appetizing in fruit salads, soups and stews, dried seeds in breads and cookies.

Start anise from seed and give it a great deal of sunlight.

(I) BASIL (*Ocimum*)

Chances are, you will grow either sweet basil (*Ocimum basilicum*) for culinary purposes, or the attractive bush basil (*O. minimum*) as a border bush. The leaves of the sweet and bush basil plants are light green, tender and smooth. Curly basil (*O. crispum*) has much larger, curly leaves. The flowers are in small but conspicuous white spikes. The whole plant is strongly aromatic. You can use the leaves of sweet basil (best for cooking) either fresh or dried in salads, vinegars, ground meats, all tomato dishes and in poultry stuffings.

Start basil from seed and make sure that it has a sunny place in which to grow.

(I) BAY (*Laurus nobilis*)

This true laurel is an evergreen shrub and can be grown outdoors as a tub plant and taken indoors in the winter. You will have to buy your first plant to begin. Although it is not very hardy, the fragrant bay is worth cultivating for its beauty. It is a lovely shade of green Its leaves are waxy and elliptical in shape. However, if you want to use bay only as a seasoning, it is best to buy the leaves commercially packaged. This plant requires a great deal of attention.

BERGAMOT, WILD (*Monarda fistulosa*)

Bergamot belongs to the mint family and this 2- to 3-foot plant grows wild in most of the United States. It has brilliant purple and red flowers, and its leaves have a pleasant lemon scent. Red bergamot (*Monarda didyma*) of the eastern states is often known as "bee balm," "Indian's plume" or "Oswego tea." Bergamot tea was used by the colonists when they refused to buy British tea.

Plants may usually be obtained from the roadside or woods.

(I) BORAGE (*Borago officinalis*)

The leaves of borage are rather rough and hairy, and since the plant tends to be straggly, you should grow it in clumps to keep it erect. It is well worth a spot in your garden for its bright blue, star-shaped flowers which bloom all summer. Use the young fresh leaves in salads, the fresh tips and the flowers in cold drinks. John Gerard's Herball (1597) suggests that borage "gives a grace to the drynkynge." Borage flowers may be candied (see page 120). A spray of cucumber-flavored borage is delicious cooked with beans, peas or cauliflower.

Borage is easily started from seed. Once established, it will self-sow; our borage has seeded itself for years.

(I) BURNET (*Sanguisorba minor*)

Salad burnet is a hardy perennial with graceful feather-shaped leaves. They are tender, cucumber flavored and excellent when used fresh in salads or vinegars. A sprig of burnet is attractive in cool drinks.

Outdoors, burnet grows erect. It is self-sowing and is difficult to transplant. Like most herbs, it needs a place in the sun. Sow seed very early in the spring.

CAMOMILE (*Anthemis nobilis*)

The English variety of camomile makes a beautiful ground cover, for it grows low and spreads gracefully over the earth. It blooms from midsummer until the first frost, producing small white and yellow daisy-shaped flowers. It has light green pinnate, or feather-shaped, leaves, and should get plenty of sun even though it does fairly well in shade. Plant seed, and camomile will self-sow from then on.

CARAWAY (*Carum carvi*)

With its delicate finely cut leaves and small creamy flowers growing in umbrels similar to Queen Anne's lace, caraway is quite lovely. Dry the seeds for use in cakes, rye bread, kraut, cabbage, pickles, cheese and stews. Bake a sprig of caraway with fruit.

It grows to about 2 feet, but if planted in the spring, it will only reach 6 to 8 inches the first year. If sown in the fall, seed may be harvested early the next year. Buy your first seed and it will self-sow thereafter.

CATNIP (*Nepeta cataria*)

Catnip produces downy, heart-shaped leaves which are green on top, grey underneath. It has purplish flowers. Catnip tea is still used medicinally, and you may also want to grow a clump of this herb for the delight of your cat.

The plant is rather weedy and does best in a rich soil without lime. Start catnip from seeds in the spring or the fall.

(I) CHERVIL (*Anthriscus cerefolium*)

For culinary use treat chervil as an annual. Even though it is really a biennial, replant it each year. Chervil produces flowers like those of miniature Queen Anne's lace, with foliage similar to parsley. If allowed to flower, chervil will set seeds in the second year of growth. If kept from flowering by cutting, the anise-flavored leaves can be used until the frost.

Start chervil from seed and give it a shady spot in which to grow.

(I) CHIVES (*Allium schoenoprasum*)

This plant is a "must," for it is delicious in any food which is enhanced by an onion taste. The slender tubular leaves of chives grow in clumps; its flowers are handsome lavender pompoms. Use chives fresh. Just cut off a few bits whenever you need them.

Start chives from bulblets or plants (from the grocery) in a rich soil and in a sunny place.

CICELY, SWEET (*Myrrhis odorata*)

Sweet cicely is often called giant sweet chervil. It has small white umbrels of flowers but it is more to be admired for its downy fernlike leaves. It has a licorice taste, similar to that of fennel. Older plants form a decorative mass of lacy foliage up to 3 feet high, a graceful background for the lower-growing herbs.

The hard, large seeds should be planted early in the fall to assure germination in the spring. Also, the roots of old plants may be divided in the spring. Sweet cicely thrives best in semi-shade.

CORIANDER (*Coriandrum sativum*)

This may have been one of the first herbs ever used in cooking. More than 5000 years ago the Chinese ate the root boiled and used the seed for flavoring. Although the seeds are unpleasant when fresh, they are delicious when dried. Use them in meats, cheeses, soups, salads and cookies. The foliage is fernlike, the pink flowers fragile.

Coriander can be started from seed and will do well as long as it gets enough sunlight.

COSTMARY (*Chrysanthemum balsamita*)

Costmary is also known as "Bible leaf" and "sweet Mary." It is hardy, a large, decorative plant with light green leaves nearly a foot long. The flowers are small and yellow; the leaves taste minty. Use them to season meat, cake and in teas.

A good background plant, growing as high as 5 feet, costmary requires thinning. It does best if partially shaded. Although you can start costmary from seed, root division is the best method of propagation.

CRESS or LAND CRESS (*Lepidum sativum*)

Garden cress is also known as "peppergrass." It does, indeed, have a peppery taste and its small dark green leaves give a nip to salads. If you have a canary, give him some garden cress.

Upland cress (*Barbarea praecox*) is a member of the mustard family. Although it is a biennial, treat it as an annual unless you are growing it to produce seed. Upland cress, which requires thinning, is much larger than garden cress, and it, too, adds a special tang to salads.

(I) DILL (*Anethum graveolens*)

This annual is characterized by its small yellow flowers arranged in umbrels and by its quickly forming seeds. Famous for their use in pickles, the seeds of dill are also excellent in sauerkraut, sauces and salads. The fine feathery leaves are also used by Europeans for flavoring.

The self-sowing dill should be sown thickly and does not require thinning. Like other herbs, it needs a great deal of sun.

FENNEL (*Foeniculum dulce*)

Sweet fennel is a beloved seasoning of Italians. You may eat the stalks raw, use the leaves with fish, the seeds with eggs, cheese, vegetables, fish and in cakes.

Foeniculum vulgare, another type of fennel, is a tall, aromatic plant which does well in almost any soil. Stems, leaves and seeds are all useful for flavoring. Fennel has bright green, feathery foliage and tiny yellow flowers in umbrels.

Start fennel from seed in a sunny spot. Although the sweet variety requires a rich soil, *F. vulgare* does better in a limy location.

23

(I) GERMANDER (*Teucrium chamaedrys*)

This hardy perennial makes a fine, attractive hedge. Its leaves are dark green and glossy and its flowers are a bright purplish-rose hue. The dwarf form (*var. prostratum*) is a good ground cover, growing to a height of about 6 inches. It is slow to start, but spreads rapidly and is particularly charming in a rock garden. The spiked pink flowers are not fragrant. Nevertheless, they are very handsome against the plant's glossy, dark green leaves. This type of germander is not very hardy and will have to be replanted every few years. Start germander from seeds, or beg some cuttings or roots from a friend.

HOREHOUND (*Marrubium vulgare*)

Horehound has been known since ancient times for its medicinal properties, and since the nineteenth century as a flavoring for candy, but only in relatively recent years has the culinary value of its leaves and flowers been recognized. It has small, oval, crinkly, greyish-green leaves. The tubular white flowers grow in whorls close to the stalk at the upper end of the stem. Both leaves and flowers may be used to season cakes, candies, sauces, meat stews and in teas.

It is becoming a weed in much of the United States and spreads rapidly by seeding and spreading roots. The bushy plant grows to about 18 inches in height. Start horehound from seed.

Hyssop (*Hyssopus officinalis*)

With its smooth, dark green leaves and blue flowers blooming from early summer until frost, hyssop makes a lovely hedge. About every 4 years, however, the plants will become scraggly and should be replaced. Remember to cut back your hyssop hedge after the first blossoms appear. This herb has a spicy, minty fragrance. You can use its leaves, stems and flowers in medicinal teas and sparingly to season vegetables and stews.

Start growing hyssop from seed sown indoors, from cuttings or by root division. It does best in partial shade.

(I) Lavender (*Lavandula spica*)

Beautiful lavender not only has a lovely aroma, but it is nice to look at, too. Its long narrow leaves are bluish-green; its flowers are blue, and the whole plant is fragrant. Valuable as an ingredient in sachets and potpourris, lavender makes an attractive hedge which will last as long as 3 years if your climate is a very warm one. In most parts of the country, however, you will have to bring it inside during the winter. *L. spica* or spike lavender is most hardy in the northern states. *L. vera* or *L. officinalis*, the English lavender, is the most fragrant.

Start lavender from young plants or root cuttings.

(I) Lemon Balm (*Melissa officinalis*)

This lemon-scented plant is wonderful for seasoning iced drinks and hot tea as well as for use in potpourris, sachets and floral bouquets. It spreads so quickly that unless you watch it closely, it will cover your entire garden. Lemon balm grows to 1½ or 2 feet tall. The oval leaves have slightly serrated edges and clusters of small, whitish flowers.

Start from seed or young plants. Lemon balm will sow itself, but a second method of propagation is by root division.

Lovage (*Levisticum officinale*)

This handsome, hardy perennial makes a good background plant, for it grows as high as 6 feet. It puts out fairly inconspicuous yellow flowers growing in umbrels and pale green, shiny, celery-like leaves. For a celery taste use the young tender leaves either fresh or dried in soups. The seeds are excellent in cakes, candies, meats and salads, and if you like, you may blanch the stems and eat them raw.

Start lovage indoors from a plant or a root which you might get from a friend or herb dealer, or sow seed early. Let lovage have a rich soil in a sunny or semi-shady place.

Marigold, Pot (*Calendula officinalis*)

This flamboyant plant puts forth bright orange and yellow flowers. It is a cheerful addition to any garden and can be used as a substitute for expensive saffron. Pot marigold should be started from seed. It is self-sowing and thrives best in rich soil.

(I) MARJORAM, SWEET (*Marjorana hortensis*)

Of the more than 30 species, *M. hortensis* is the most valuable for kitchen use. The leaves are similar to oregano in taste and may be used either fresh or dried. They are small, greyish-green in color and quite pungent.

Start marjoram from seeds sown indoors, from stem cuttings or crown division. It does best in a warm, moist, light chalky soil, and you will have to keep it cut back to inhibit its woody growth. If your climate is relatively cold, treat marjoram as an annual.

(I) MINT

Of the more than 40 mints the most popular are: peppermint (*Mentha piperita*); spearmint (*M. spicata*); wooly mint (*M. rotundifolia*); variegated applemint (*M. gentilis variegata*). All the mints are zesty and extremely useful for culinary purposes—hot teas, cold drinks, jellies, sauces and candies. They are easy to grow and must be restrained as they spread rapidly. To get them started, buy or beg a root or a plant. They need lots of moisture.

Nasturtium (*Tropaeolum minus*)

The nasturtium is well known for its bright, showy flowers. The dwarf variety (*T. minus*) makes a pretty border. Use its petals in teas and salads. *T. majus* is the larger or climbing variety. The leaves of both varieties are round, tender and peppery, delicious in salads.

Start nasturtiums from seed. Like other herbs they need a sunny place in which to live.

Oregano

Oregano, the well-known herb so essential in Italian cookery, is actually wild marjoram. The type which grows in the United States is inferior in quality, however, and you will not want to grow it yourself. The dried oregano sold in stores may be of any number of species. Choose the one with the taste and scent that most pleases you.

(I) Parsley (*Petroselinum hortense*)

This biennial should be treated as an annual. The familiar foliage can be used the first year. If undisturbed through the winter, seeds will form the second year, but the leaves will not have as good a taste as the first year. Parsley is very slow to germinate, but grows rapidly once it has come up, and will be good even after a few light frosts. You may want to grow both the curly- and flat-leafed varieties; the former for its appearance, the latter for its taste. The curly-leafed parsley makes a very charming border.

Sow parsley seed in drills or light furrows. Later, thin the plants so that each will have about 4 inches in which to grow. Parsley thrives in either sunlight or partial shade.

PENNYROYAL (*Mentha pulegium*)

Although actually a mint, pennyroyal grows prostrate rather than erect as do other mints. It is the smallest of the mints. Unlike spearmint, it does not spread and therefore does not need to be confined. A hardy perennial, it is attractive for its furry, small oval leaves and bluish-lavender whorls of flowers.

Pennyroyal tastes like other mints, but is rather strong. Our grandmothers called it "pennyrile" or "pudding grass" and used it in cooking, but today pennyroyal is grown only for its usefulness as a ground cover.

Buy roots or plants and then propagate by root division. Select a partially shady spot for its home.

(I) ROSE GERANIUM (*Pelargonium graveolens*)

Rose geranium is a perennial which is quite sensitive to cold and must be brought indoors during the winter. It is famous for its use in jellies and cakes, in sachets and potpourris.

Get stem cuttings from a friend or buy a plant. It rarely blooms but is wonderfully fragrant.

(I) ROSEMARY (*Rosmarinus officinalis*)

The most widely known herb of history and folklore, rosemary resembles an evergreen. Its leaves look like long oval pine needles, even more so when dried to preserve their warm, pungent spicy taste. Rosemary is a tender perennial which you must bring inside during the winter. Shrubs will grow from 3 to 5 feet tall outdoors, but grown as a house plant, rosemary will probably be less than a foot high and will trail its lower branches gracefully over the sides of the pot.

Although it is possible to start rosemary from seed, it is safer to buy a plant about a foot high. Propagate by stem cuttings or layering. Rosemary does best with abundant sunlight, in a thin, gravelly soil.

RUE (*Ruta graveolens*)

In medieval times rue was used to season salads, fish and eggs, but it has a somewhat unpleasant aroma and its taste is no longer much liked. It has also been used as a medicinal herb, but be careful; some people develop a rash when handling this plant.

Rue provides an extremely pretty border or low hedge, having bluish-green divided leaves and gay yellow flowers. Start from seed or get cuttings or roots.

(I) SAGE (*Salvia officinalis*)

Sage is perhaps our best known herb. There are 500 species of which a large number have either a medicinal or culinary value. *S. officinalis* is the one used for the Thanksgiving turkey dressing. Three other common varieties of sage are: *S. rutilans*, "pineapple" sage; *S. sclarea*, clary; *S. splendend*, the common red salvia used in flower gardens.

Sage's grey-green soft, furry leaves are attractive. Cut the bush back after the blue flowers are gone. Put the plant in a corner where it can remain undisturbed.

Start sage from seed. It may be propagated from root division, cuttings or layering. It thrives in a poor soil if it gets plenty of sun.

SANTOLINA OR LAVENDER COTTON (*Santolina chamaecyparissus*)

Santolina is sometimes known as French lavender. A fragrant, small plant, with soft grey, fine foliage, it is very decorative. The button-like discs of flowers are yellow. Formerly it was used as a moth repellent and packed with clothing. Now it is grown as an ornamental plant. Except for the color of its leaves, it is not at all similar to lavender in spite of its name. A bush may grow to 6 feet across, making santolina a favorite edging for knot gardens.

Start it from plants and let it grow in a sunny spot.

(I) SAVORY (*Satureia hortensis*)

A fragrant, shrubby plant with small, narrow downy leaves and tiny flowers ranging from pink to purple, savory is a valuable addition to any garden. Summer savory has the best flavor, similar to that of marjoram although stronger and more aromatic. The dried leaves are particularly good with beans, in soups, stews and ground meats. Of the 130 to 140 known species of savory, winter savory, *S. montana*, is also worth cultivating. It is not as fine a culinary herb as summer savory, but you can use it discreetly.

Since the seed of savory does not germinate well, start it from root cuttings. Let savory have a great deal of sunlight and a fairly poor soil.

SORREL, GARDEN (*Rumex acetosa*)

Sorrel dates back more than 4000 years. It is sometimes called "sour grass" because of the acid taste of the large fleshy leaves. These broad leaves, arrow-shaped at the base, give a tang to salads. The greenish flowers grow on tall spikes. Sorrel usually grows from one to two feet in height. It is easily started from seed.

TANSY (*Tanacetum vulgare*)

A strewing herb of medieval times, tansy was also formerly used in cakes and puddings eaten at Easter, and it was dried for teas. Cookbooks of the 16th and 17th centuries included recipes calling for tansy, but today it is grown only as a background plant. It attains a height of about 4 feet, has fernlike leaves and flowers which resemble small yellow buttons.

Since it spreads naturally in the manner of a weed, sow tansy in a relatively empty corner of your yard or garden. It will grow in either sun or shade.

(I) TARRAGON (*Artemisia dracunculus*)

A. dracunculus is the only true tarragon. Fresh or dried, the leaves are an excellent seasoning for vinegar, fish, poultry and salads. For its appearance and its superior taste, tarragon is an aristocrat among herbs.

Since true tarragon does not set seed in America, you will have to start with a plant. Propagate by cuttings or root division. Each plant requires much sunlight and about a foot of space in which to grow. If you do not bring tarragon indoors during the winter, you should cover it well with leaves. Since true tarragon plants are difficult to obtain, you may decide that growing it yourself is not worth the trouble. In that case, you can buy commercially packaged tarragon.

(I) THYME (*Thymus vulgaris*)

There are more than 60 varieties of thyme, but *T. vulgaris* is the best for culinary purposes. Its greyish, arrow-shaped leaves spread rapidly; its flowers are attractive. If you would like to collect many species of one herb, the thymes would be a good choice. *T. serpyllum*, "lemon thyme," makes a charming fragrant ground cover, for it is low-growing and spreads quickly.

Start seeds of thyme indoors before transplanting the seedlings to your yard. Propagate by cuttings or layering. Although thyme is hardy, it should be protected during the winter by a covering of leaves, and it requires a great deal of sun.

WOODRUFF, SWEET (*Asperula odorata*)

This plant is especially popular because it will grow in the shade. The foliage is hay-scented, the entire plant fragrant. Sweet woodruff has light green leaves which grow in whorls of 7 to 9 and tiny white flowers arranged in flat clusters. It makes a very charming border plant. Its penetrating sweetness is released when it is crushed.

Seeds should be fresh and sown in cold frames indoors; then transplant the seedlings outside where they will self-sow in the future. You can also get new plants by root division. Sweet woodruff grows wild in shady woods.

3. Preparing Your Outdoor Herb Garden

Be lazy and love it! You might call that my gardening motto.

There is a garden club called "Plant and Pray" and that name pretty well sums up my system. If a plant could sigh, it would do so when I put it in the ground. But, fortunately for me, herbs are the friendliest, the most adaptable of all plants. Most herbs love sun, but will grow in partial shade. Of course they need some sunshine to develop their fragrant oils, and if they get too little sun, their flavor will not be so good.

The herbs do not overly care whether their soil is poor or rich. In fact, rich soil will produce large leaves, but relatively little fragrance and flavor. Unless you want herbs for looks alone, do not use much fertilizer. Although a light loam is preferable, our own herbs must grow in clay. And they do. We have always garnered all the herbs we and our friends can use.

The actual planting of your herb garden is a simple matter. The next chapter gives you ideas for planning and laying out your garden so you can best utilize whatever space you have available. But whether you have your herbs all gathered together in one small patch, or spread out over a large area, there are some basic planting procedures to follow.

Most seeds may be sown directly in the garden in spring. When planting seeds outdoors for new plants to bring in for the kitchen window, try to get them in the soil by mid-summer. By fall the plants should be well established in the pots and boxes in which they are to grow during the winter, so that they will not have to undergo the shock of transplanting at the same time as the change from outdoor to indoor living. If your growing season is short, or if you wish to start using your herbs early in the summer, it is best to start some seeds in flats indoors even before the warm weather sets in. If you do not have the space or time for starting your own flats, you can usually buy seedlings or small plants from a nursery or seed company.

Preparing the Soil

If you are starting your herb garden outdoors in the spring, here are some simple directions.

First, plan where each variety is to go. Remember that the perennials must stay in their original positions for longer than a year. Arrange them so that they will not be disturbed, and so that the taller plants will not overshadow the smaller herbs. It is wise to plant the thick, heavy-leaved varieties requiring the least moisture—sage, thyme, winter savory, marjoram—in one part of the bed, and those which need more frequent watering in another.

Good drainage is a special requirement of herbs. Even those such as the mints, which love water, do not like to stand with their feet in a puddle. A gentle slope is the best place for your garden if the soil is not naturally porous. In Elizabethan times, many herb gardens were raised above ground level, with boards, rocks or other materials filled in with earth to make a raised bed

The herb bed should be spaded to a depth of 6 to 10 inches. Spade bone meal or lime in with some well-rotted manure, and pulverize the soil to the full depth. For the thymes, lavender, rosemary, and burnet, mix old, well-broken plaster into the soil. The mints, tarragon, lovage, and angelica will appreciate a fairly rich bed of loam and compost, although they, too, like a slightly alkaline soil.

For your small herb patches, you can get your lime free by digging in crumbled eggshells around the roots of plants, or adding bits of pulverized plaster (perhaps from a house that is being torn down) or wood ashes. If you do not want to bother with any of these, buy hydrated lime and add one pound to a 5- by 12-foot area. If you are starting a new herb garden in the spring, add the lime at that time. Then add more lime in the fall, but keep it away from the perennials.

If the soil is extremely poor, growth will be slow, the leaves tough and the flavor bitter, so add some humus in the form of manure or compost. If you do not have access to either of these, you can buy good commercial fertilizer at little cost. Most herbs, however, do thrive in rather poor, rocky soil as long as it is kept loose. After adding the fertilizer or lime, rake the soil well until it is fine and smooth.

Sowing the Seed

Most annuals are started from seed sown in the garden. As for biennials, you may grow them just as you do annuals. You can buy many varieties of herb seed at your seed store, nursery or supermarket, but you cannot always be sure of what you are getting. For example, tarragon may be in the seed rack but it is not a true tarragon and is hardly worth planting. True tarragon does not set seed in this country, so it is necessary to buy plants. Then there is basil. I bought "sweet basil" and got the "great ocimum sweet basil." Later, I bought another packet with the same label, same brand. It turned out to be "small ocimum bush basil." Now I save and plant my own basil seeds, so I can be sure what variety I'm planting. But don't worry. Except for tarragon and basil, commercially packaged seeds are reliable

Mix small seeds like those of marjoram or thyme with fine sand so that they can be distributed uniformly. This is not necessary for larger seeds. No matter where you are planting, always soak slow-germinating seeds in warm water for several hours or overnight. You will learn which are slow-germinating by reading the instructions on the seed packets.

Most of the seeds are so tiny that I broadcast, or scatter, them within the bounds of the lines that I have drawn in the soil. Sometimes I make shallow furrows with a finger tip or twig and space the seeds in these as well as I can. Herbs will come up fairly thickly, and that is fine. One of the many delightful things about herbs is that they have flavor practically from the moment that they stick their little tips through the ground. You can use them as soon as they are large enough to thin out.

After sowing, take a handful of crumbled soil and sprinkle it very lightly over the fine seeds. One-sixteenth of an inch is deep enough for small ones, but the larger seeds may be covered a bit deeper. Moisten the ground lightly to keep the seeds in place. Wooden stakes about a foot high should be put at intervals along the rows or around the edges of the beds to hold sheets of heavy plastic above the tender seedlings. The plastic canopies will protect the new plants from hard rains. When the weather is fine, it is a good idea to remove the plastic overnight to help the tiny plants toughen. When the seedlings are well started, remove the plastic permanently.

Seeds, and later, seedlings should be watered only when the soil seems quite dry.

Planting in Flats, Pots or Boxes

Herbs are like people. They need light and air, food and water, a little attention, but not too much coddling. Some must be started indoors, chiefly because in most parts of the country the growing season is rather short. Perennials are better started indoors in cold frames or flats from either seeds or cuttings, and the plants set in the garden in late spring. But if you prefer, you can buy young plants at a nursery. After they are well established, you can propagate your own as described in Chapter 5.

There are a few things which you will need to know about starting seeds in flats, pots or boxes. To me this is the only tedious part of herb growing, and come March, I'm envious of those who live in sunny climes. Still, if you want more than a half a dozen varieties of herbs, you must learn to cultivate seedlings.

As for seed planters, you don't have to buy a thing. Berry and other small fruit or vegetable boxes lined with foil, coffee cans, milk cartons cut crosswise—all are excellent for raising seedlings. Small flats are much more convenient to handle and store than are larger ones. Now on the market are excellent small portable greenhouses for starting seedlings. They control the humidity and temperature and act as neat and dependable baby sitters for your tiny seedlings.

A good standard seeding mixture consists of 2 parts of good garden loam, 1 part leaf mold or peat moss, and 1 part sharp sand. Since herbs need an alkaline mixture, 1 quart of ground limestone or well-crushed plaster, 1 pint of bone meal and 2 quarts of well-rotted manure should be added to each bushel of the mixture. If you do not wish to make up this mixture, peat moss or sterile vermiculite mixed with a little sand is especially good. Be sure you wet the vermiculite mixture thoroughly. Fill each container for seeds within a half inch of the top.

Sow seeds on the surface and then cover with a thin layer of dirt or sand. Punch a few holes in a piece of clear plastic and cover the containers. The ventilated plastic bags in which oranges and potatoes are packed make good coverings, and you can slip a whole flat inside of one of them. To hold it firmly, tuck the open end under the flat. Another good covering is the jug greenhouse illustrated on page 41. Try this for a miniature hothouse. It isn't my original idea; I saw it at a flower show, and adopted it. You start with a gallon vinegar or cider jug. Cut off the bottom—you know how, with a string wrapped around, set afire, and plunged into cold water. Put the jug over the can or box of newly planted seeds. Leave the lid off the jug for circulation of air.

For fine seed, moisten the soil well and press down evenly in pots or flats with a small board or brick. Make shallow depressions with the edge of a thin board or ruler and sift the seeds thinly into the grooves. Press them down with a board and cover very thinly with fine sand. Plastic bags or the jug hothouse will prevent the seeds from drying out before germination begins. However, if the soil *does* dry out, put the flats or pots into water up to half their height until thoroughly moistened. The water should be absorbed upward from the bottom so that the seeds will not be disturbed. If only the top of the earth seems dry, water lightly. Do not

let the soil get soaking wet. For spraying the seeds and later for watering the seedlings, a clothes sprinkling bottle is ideal.

Feed the seedlings sparingly with liquid fertilizer when they begin to sprout. After you have transferred them to larger pots or outdoors, a feeding once every two weeks will be sufficient.

Seeds will not need light until they poke their little noses above the surface of the earth. When this happens, give them a warm window in which to grow. Temperature should be from 60° to 70° Fahrenheit until the seeds sprout, then 55° to 65° is best. Seedlings need fresh air too so leave a window near the boxes open a crack. You will have to watch the temperature carefully. If the new plants get too much sun, move the planters back from the window a little. On the other hand, if the sprouts seem spindly, they probably are not getting enough light. Be sure to turn the containers every day or so to keep the plants from growing lopsided. You can use fluorescent or incandescent lighting if necessary. If you use artificial lights, however, do not leave them on for longer than 14 to 16 hours a day as most plants need a period of darkness.

"Damping-off" is the greatest hazard in growing seedlings. This fungus disease attacks the stems of young seedlings just where they emerge from the earth, and causes them to rot and break off. It is caused by too much moisture.

Cuttings

In general, the method for starting cuttings is the same as that for seedlings. A large plastic box makes a good rooting box for cuttings. Punch a few drainage holes in the bottom and fill the box with two inches of vermiculite. Wet it down thoroughly and insert your cuttings, from which you have trimmed the leaves from the lower two inches.

Cover the box with a sheet of plastic and either cut a few air holes or prop up the sides of the plastic so that they will hang loosely. Put the box in a light place out of direct sunlight. When new leaves appear, you will know that roots have formed. The cuttings are then ready to be transferred to small pots of soil.

Training Your Seedlings to Live Outdoors

Plants started in the house are more tender than those started outdoors because of the higher temperatures and greater protection to which they have become accustomed. If the young plants are set out in the garden while the nights are still chilly, their growth will be checked. The youngsters cannot easily adapt to the sudden changes. If you start plants in cold frames, the hardening off process is simple. Open the sash a crack for a short time each day, gradually increasing the length of time. After 10 or 12 days, the sash may be left off.

If you start seedlings in flats, it may be necessary to take them outdoors during the day and return them to the house or potting shed for the night until they are well established and the nights are warm.

Transplanting Your Seedlings

When the seedlings have two pairs of leaves, they can be transplanted. Before moving them from their flats or boxes to a permanent location, water them thoroughly. A calm

Seedlings raised in long narrow boxes are easy to remove for transplanting. If you use a milk carton, cut down one side, slice apart between plants, and the sections will slip out easily.

Milk cartons cut crosswise make excellent planters for seedlings. Place them close together in a box.

Set each seedling in a hole large enough so that the roots are not crowded. Push the earth back into the hole and firm around the plant.

Seedling pots made of paper may be set directly in the ground.

A newspaper tent protects seedlings. Be sure to weight the tent so that it will not blow away or injure the young plants.

Commercial hot caps provide more protection if you plant early, before the weather is warm.

cloudy day is best for transplanting. At least, do not set the delicate little seedlings into their new home when the sun is high. Transplant as late in the evening as the light will allow so that the night dew will settle on the seedlings.

Lift each plant with a tongue depressor or small stick and lower the roots into the holes you have already made in the soil. If possible, lift out an undisturbed chunk of dirt around the roots of each plant as you remove it from its box or flat. Set each plant far enough down into its new home so that its first pair of leaves is flush with the soil. Pack the earth around it, and then flood it with as much water as if will absorb. Leave plenty of space; since they will soon need all the sun and air they can get, seedlings should never be crowded.

When the small plants are finally in their permanent positions in the garden, they should be protected from the hot sun for a few days with "hot caps" (see the illustration on page 43), newspaper tents, plastic canopies or shingles. Be careful to weight down papers with rocks or clods so that they will not blow away or fall onto the young plants.

When Winter Comes

Before severe weather sets in, trim back by one-third the perennials which are to remain in the garden. These bits and snips of herbs need not be wasted. Freeze or dry them as described in Chapter 7 and add them to your winter's store.

Tuck dry leaves among and around the small delicate branches of the perennial herbs. Oak leaves are especially good, since they will not mat and rot. Light twiggy branches will hold the leaves in place. Lilac branches are good, as are old evergreens. You may add more leaves as the temperature drops.

When the ground freezes, cover the more tender perennials with inverted baskets loosely filled with leaves. Some, like thyme and marjoram, live through fairly severe weather without this extra protection.

There will come a night when a killing frost will lay low your herbs, and then you should cut down the mint, costmary, chives, sorrel, lovage and sweet cicely. Do not cut the lemon balm, sage, thyme or other woody plants until spring. There have been years when I was sure that I lost my bed of thyme, and was tempted to uproot it late in the spring. But so far, at least some of it has finally put out new green shoots. So be patient about it.

Mulch the thyme and mint lightly. Often a natural covering of leaves will be enough. When I rake the lawn for the final time, I put a few armloads of leaves on the herbs.

Although most perennials can be left outside if protected, you may want to bring plants of these indoors: rosemary, lemon verbena, rose geranium, tarragon, mint, chives, lemon balm. Make them part of your indoor herb garden, described in Chapter 8.

Spring Comes Again

In the spring the perennial herbs will begin to put forth new shoots as soon as the first warm rays of the sun hit them. It is safest to pamper the delicate new growth a bit until it becomes hardened to the elements. Remove the protective covering gradually, but replace it in the evenings when the nights are cool. This is when the plastic cover described on page 42 is convenient. You can put it on and take it off easily, and vary the length of exposure according to each day's temperature. When the herbs are growing well again and no longer need their protective coverings, the most exacting part of your work is over.

Spring is also the time to replenish your garden by sowing annuals (anise, basil, borage and dill, for example) and by replacing any perennials which failed to survive the winter.

An herb's way of sprouting with an ingrown flavor is very helpful when you complete your herb garden for the new year. A taste will tell you which little green shoots are herbs and which are weeds, and you will not have to guess which perennials need to be resown.

If the weather is dry, the plants should be watered well in the evening. Wet them thoroughly, for if the water does not soak deeply, it may do more harm than good. The surface will dry and bake, and the roots will not receive any moisture. Thyme, marjoram, winter savory and rosemary in particular needs lots of water.

Probably you will not have to do much weeding. As I have confessed, I am a lazy gardener. If I had to cultivate and weed continuously, much of the joy would be gone. I just pull a few weeds each day. In spite of this neglect, my herbs do grow. Not so vigorously as some, perhaps. But we can scarcely tear down our neighbors' house and hedge to get more light, so we pick the spot which gets the most sun in the morning; the little plants must make do. And they thrive!

Because of bad growing conditions, my herbs do not grow very luxuriantly, and so they do not need the pinching back, the thinning and the other attention that a more perfect growth would require. Still, we have all the herbs we can use—to garner or to give away. That's why I say, "Plant what you want, where you can, and have fun!"

4. Where Does Your Garden Grow?

Even if you have only a tiny back yard, you needn't deprive yourself of an outdoor herb garden. If you have a great deal of space, how lucky you are!

We have three herb gardens, and I hope that you, too, will plant more than one. If one is good, several are better. You wouldn't plant flowers in only one bit of ground when they could brighten up so many other places as well. This is also true of herbs.

Now here are a few specific suggestions. Do have a clump of chives and an edging of parsley handy at the kitchen door. Mint is a "natural" for circling the bird bath, where it will be sprinkled by the cheerful splashing of robins and sparrows. Put some of the bushier herbs into your vegetable garden. Basil, germander, parsley, rosemary, rue, sage, and lavender make attractive borders or low hedges for beds of vegetables, flowers or other herbs. If you live in a warm climate, your lavender hedge may live for as long as three years. Parsley makes a delightful edging for a flower bed. Even if you grow lemon balm, burnet, caraway, coriander, dill, dittany, rose geranium, mint or marjoram indoors as houseplants, there's no reason you can't *also* grow these herbs outdoors.

If you would like a good ground cover, the *T. serphyllum* variety of thyme spreads rapidly and is low-growing. It is lovely between stepping stones or around a pool. When touched, it releases a delightful fragrance. Also good for this purpose are the fernlike camomile, germander (var. *Prostratum*) with its thick, glossy leaves and pink flowers, and the lovely, hay-scented sweet woodruff. These are old-fashioned herbs, well known and popular among gardeners of colonial days.

47

Usually, a space 5 x 12 feet will grow enough of the basic culinary herbs for your family. Annual flavoring herbs (for example, basil and summer savory) do not require much space. When grown for a season's use only, six plants of each will furnish enough seasoning for an average-sized family. But if you plan to dry some leaves for sachets, teas or seasoning, plant twice this many.

You can plant herbs in decorative jardinieres to line your terrace or walk, lay them out in formal patterns in a knot garden, set them along fences or walls, and scatter them among your vegetables. These ideas will bring fun, variety and added interest to your herb gardening.

No matter what specific spots you choose, do have some herbs near your house. Much of the fun is in running out as the fancy strikes you to gather a leaf here, a sprig there.

On Your Terrace or Walk

If you have long dreamed of growing your own herbs, lack of garden space need not hold you back. Start with large pots—those which, because of their size, cannot be moved about or brought indoors. Use a row of these jardinieres as a border for either the front or back walk. They are attractive even when empty. If you want to plant tarragon, which likes space, it will thrive in one of these pots. You can put sage, rosemary, bushy sweet basil, lemon balm or any of the mints in pots 12 inches or larger.

If you have a permanent terrace planter of brick, stone or cement built against the house where it is protected, it is an ideal place for perennials. Chives, thyme, mint, sage and winter savory, for example, will survive through the winter if they are mulched lightly. To protect chives, lightly pile leaves over them, and you will have green shoots to snip almost before the snow disappears in the spring. If your planter is built directly on the ground, even those herbs with long taproots, such as lovage and parsley, will thrive in it.

On a fairly long paved terrace try a checkerboard effect at one end, leaving alternate squares open for planting. This is an excellent location either for those herbs which you use most often in the kitchen, or for those which, like the mints, need confining.

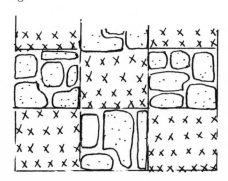

A similar idea is to place your checkerboard herb patch near your movable charcoal grill or outdoor fireplace. There you can grow those herbs which you will use in barbecuing as well as in iced drinks.

An oversized pot or a wooden tub by the kitchen door will hold a clump of chives, two or three parsley plants, basil, one or two marjoram plants and two or three plants of thyme. Savory, lemon balm and spearmint are worth adding. These will take you through a culinary year very nicely. If you wish to include all of these, of course two tubs will be necessary.

One tub and a group of six or eight large pots will also make an attractive, space-saving arrangement. Winter savory, thyme, burnet, basil and other herbs could have individual pots.

To add color to your terrace, pot some of those flowers which are also classified as herbs. You can have your flowers and eat them too, if you grow nasturtiums, calendulas or pot marigolds. By all means include a rose geranium tricked out with some artificial geranium blooms. The rose-scented geranium does not generally blossom and when it does, the flowers are inconspicuous.

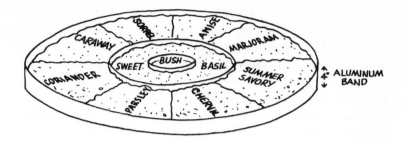

A lazy-Susan effect is interesting on your terrace, porch or in your yard. Surround a tall potted plant such as a bush of rosemary or scented geranium with any number of smaller potted plants.

A strawberry jar (a large pottery jar with "pockets" on the sides) makes a delightful herb garden, as does a barrel with holes bored in its sides. These can be placed almost anywhere—in the yard, at the corners of the terrace, or even on either side of a doorway. You might be happier with jars rather than barrels at the front door, however.

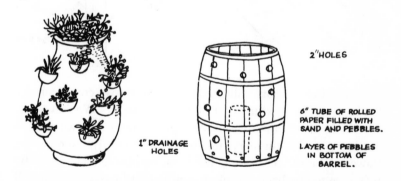

A strawberry jar is delightfully decorative at an entryway. Include some of those fabulous plastic flowers which people must touch in order to find out whether they are real. The plastic will withstand sun and rain, and you can get a colorful effect by tucking a few of these flowers among the herbs.

You can grow pots of herbs on the window sill or on a narrow ledge in 5-inch pots, but do not try a smaller size than this. If your window sill will not take pots of at least 5 inches, you can get small shelves to attach to the sill. These not only provide space for larger pots, but also leave room for the plants to spread. Chives will do fairly well in the 5-inch pots; so will small plants of winter savory, mint, thyme, sweet marjoram, basil, rosemary, lemon balm and burnet.

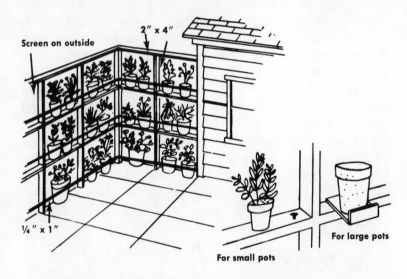

Any window box will make an attractive container for herbs or for a mixture of herbs and flowers. We have one to which we transplant our rose geranium when we take it outdoors each summer; it flourishes mightily among the flowers. Since geraniums need to be disciplined severely, it is wise to cut back the plant well before frost, so that it will start growing again before you bring it indoors.

If you plant in a window box, bore some holes in the bottom and place a layer of coarse gravel under the soil. Cover the drainage holes with pieces of broken flower pots or broken crockery topped with a thin layer of gravel.

Although herbs generally are sun worshippers, this is less true of those plants grown in containers than of those in your garden. Pots or boxes set on a paved terrace dry out quickly from the combined effects of wind and reflected sun. See that potted plants are watered daily and, if possible, keep them in a spot which is shaded part of the day. If they are planted in full sunlight, either move them during the hottest part of the day, or give them the temporary shelter of a beach umbrella or an awning.

When potted plants are well established, after 3 or 4 weeks, it is time to begin feeding them. Use a good commercial fertilizer. Someone at your supply store will be glad to recommend one if you do not already have a favorite. The best rule is to follow the directions on the package.

Some herbs will thrive happily from season to season in the same pot. Others will become crowded and will have to be repotted. The mints, which propagate by means of underground stems, may become pot-bound. Herbs which have long taproots, such as parsley or lovage, may also outgrow their pots.

Tarragon does best if repotted after 6 months. It may be divided at that time. You can also start new plants from the mint which you have divided.

The Formal Garden

You do not need to wear a 12th-century costume, sing madrigals or plant a knot garden in order to grow herbs. However, a simple design will add greatly to the beauty and interest of your plot. You will enjoy a small formal herb garden, even though you plant herbs in several other locations as well.

Intricate knot gardens were made hundreds of years ago and became famous in the days of the Renaissance. They are supposed to have gotten their name from the gardeners' habit of taking designs from embroidery patterns. Geometric circles, curves and angles, interlocked rings and diamonds, crosses and ladders were used. Many of the designs were rich in religious or pagan symbolism.

The outlines of the pattern were carried out with grey-green santolina, dwarf lavender bushes, clipped rosemary or other bushy plants which either do not grow too tall, or which can be kept clipped. Such elaborate mazes were laid out in the 1600's that on some large grounds, guards were stationed in towers to prevent guests from losing their way among hedges which grew more than head-high. The ordinary maze, however, was edged with such low-growing shrubs as southernwood, rosemary, lavender, rue, marjoram and basil, rather than with the taller hedges.

The first knot garden which I knew well was just inside the gate leading to a large university. We played there as children, and the gardener let us pick the sweet violets which grew in wide beds beyond the lavender. Oh, those fragrant hedges! When he clipped them, we gathered up armloads of sweet lavender and carried them home to put in the linen closet and among our handkerchiefs and hair ribbons.

In that particular garden, the path would suddenly widen to a circle which enclosed a bed of bright flowers. From there it would branch off in several directions, and we were fond of pretending that we were lost in its maze. That garden, alas, long ago fell victim to progress.

There is no doubt about it; herbs look best in a formal setting. But do not make the mistake of thinking that "formal" need mean "intricate." A very simple design can be lovely. I am going to give you a few, both formal and informal, to help set your imagination to work.

Just what to plant in each area is entirely up to you, for if I should say, "Put your rosemary here, your basil there, and a bush of hyssop in the center," your own plan might be ruined. Perhaps you cannot get a hyssop plant, and your

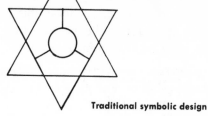

rosemary may not have come up this year. So there you are with nothing except basil! And lovely as it is, basil alone will not make an herb garden.

Look at these plans and choose those which will best fit your space. Then, having bought your packets of seeds and checked as to available plants, decide what is to go where.

If you are planning a knot garden or one with a special design, you may not wish to plant it the first spring that you begin growing herbs. It is a major project, and you will need plenty of time for carrying out your plan.

Traditional maze

However, you should decide now where you want to locate your formal garden. It would be pleasant to have it in view of the house or terrace. Choose this location most carefully of all, for it is apt to be permanent. During the summer you can work on it as you have time.

Try to visualize the mature plants. Remember that shrubs and plants will grow and grow and grow. How many times have you been irritated by bushes and even trees planted so close to a walk that you could scarcely pass? Herbs, too, spread. If they are not divided and thinned, they will soon take over more than their allotted space. Even though seedlings of different herbs may be the same size when you plant them, they will not remain that way when full grown. Angelica will tower over the marjoram, for example, should you have been so indiscreet as to have planted it in the foreground.

If the garden is to be large enough to need paths, lay them out. Bricks or flat stones are good, or you can make your own paving blocks by pouring cement into molds. The man who runs your seed store or nursery probably will be glad to tell you how to do it. If you cannot use bricks, stones or paving blocks, gravel paths will do, although they will be more trouble in the long run because they must be constantly raked and replenished.

Next spring your formal garden should be ready for planting.

Traditional knot garden

Variations of traditional garden

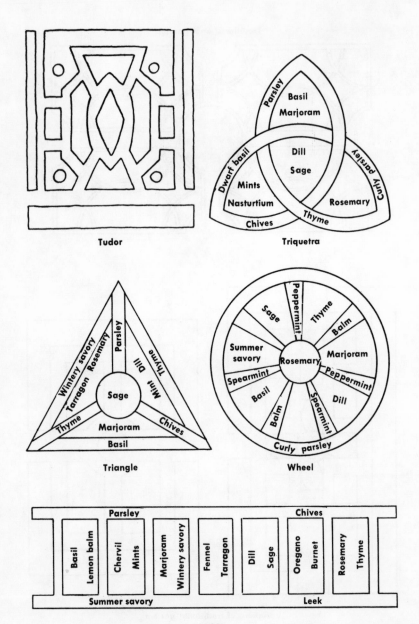

Tudor

Triquetra

Parsley

Basil

Marjoram

Dwarf basil

Dill

Sage

Curly parsley

Mints

Nasturtium

Rosemary

Chives

Thyme

Triangle

Wintery savory

Tarragon Rosemary

Parsley

Mint Dill

Thyme

Sage

Thyme

Marjoram

Chives

Basil

Wheel

Peppermint

Sage

Thyme

Summer savory

Balm

Rosemary

Marjoram

Spearmint

Peppermint

Basil

Dill

Balm

Spearmint

Curly parsley

Ladder

Parsley

Chives

Basil

Lemon balm

Chervil

Mints

Marjoram

Wintery savory

Fennel

Tarragon

Dill

Sage

Oregano

Burnet

Rosemary

Thyme

Summer savory

Leek

Other Spots for Herbs

Here are some unusual ways to display your herbs. An old wheelbarrow will hold quite a few plants, and you can easily move it from sun to shade as the need arises. You may want to wheel it into your basement playroom when winter comes.

If you have a sun dial, a bird bath, a gazing ball or a small statue in your yard, plant a wheel of herbs around it, leaving from two to four narrow paths leading up to the central object. This arrangement is particularly attractive with the beds edged with bricks or low fencing.

Do you have a lamp post in your yard? Day or night, it will show off your herb garden. Plant herbs around the base of the light, then let a morning glory, a hop vine or any other attractive climber use the pole.

Don't forget to plant by fences and walls. One of my dearest dreams is to have a walled garden. If you are fortunate enough to have one, I hope that you grow herbs in the crannies or at the base. A fence provides a wonderful long space to be lined with pots.

No ground space? You can grow a surprising number of herbs in tiers along a fence or wall.

Herbs are fine plantings for the crevices between bricks or stones of paths or in a rock garden. Although tender herbs cannot survive trampling feet, the thymes (particularly *T. albus, T. coccineus, T. Annie K. Hall, T. britannicus, T. lanuginous* and *T. pulchellus*) are good for such spots. Corsican mint (*Mentha requieni*), too, will live between stones, but the following year you will have to search out its seedlings and put them back where you want them. The original plants tend to winter-kill or die, and the new shoots will pop up almost anywhere.

Herbs for edging should be low compact shrubs. Hyssop is ideal. Rue, santolina, white sage, rosemary and box are also good for this purpose. But easier to come by and equally attractive as edgings are parsley, marjoram and bush basil.

If you have a vegetable garden, there is no reason why you should not plant some herbs there. Because of the small size and poor soil of our back yard, we plant herbs with the vegetables in a garden which is located at some distance from the house. These are the "quantity" herbs—that is, those which take more space than we have in the herb garden proper, or of which we want plenty to harvest for drying. Parsley makes a beautiful border for our vegetable garden. In one corner are two bush basil plants. Sage grows there, too, as does the prolific dill which we allow to self-sow.

Now it is your turn. By this time you should have ideas enough for half a hundred herb gardens. Never again can you say, "I want to plant some herbs when we have the space." The space is there; you will find it if you look.

5. Learn to Multiply and Divide Your Herbs

One of the many pleasant things about herbs is that, once started, they will cooperate with you in propagating themselves. Except for some annuals, you will seldom need to buy seeds or plants after your first investment.

The general methods of propagation are by seed, runners, layering, stem cuttings, bulblets, root division, crown division and root crown division.

Since viable seed—seed capable of growing and developing —is almost unobtainable from some herbs, such as true tarragon, it is necessary to understand some of the alternative methods of keeping your herb plants renewed.

Propagating from roots and stems rather than from seed will better maintain the particular strain you want, once you have found it. For instance, sage with desirable qualities often will not come true when seeded. So cuttings are safest for sage. Cuttings are also desirable for woody plants such as lavender, winter savory and thyme.

Chives may be started from seed, but dividing the bulblets is a much quicker way, and is easier than seeding. Garden mints very rarely set seed, but applemint, spearmint and peppermint can be started easily by runners. Lemon balm also propagates by runners and self-sows readily.

Quite a few other plants will self-sow their seeds. But this is not a dependable method, especially if your garden is small, because you must keep each herb confined to its allotted space. When an herb cannot remain undisturbed from year to year, you may dig the self-sown seeds under and lose them. Or you may find seedlings popping up many feet from the original bed, and perhaps fail to recognize them in time to transplant them to the place where they should be.

The methods of propagating individual herbs are given in the chart on page 128, and in the list on pages 16–34.

Layering

Layering is a simple method of propagating such herbs as thyme and sage. These two may layer themselves, but you can do it for them and others by pegging down a stem of a growing plant in the soft earth. Cover the section with soil and water it daily. When a good root growth appears on the buried stem, cut it away from the parent plant. Spring is the time for layering.

If you are one of those thrifty people who wonder what to do with extra wire coat hangers, I can tell you one use for them. Cut them into short lengths and bend to make staples for pegging down stems when layering.

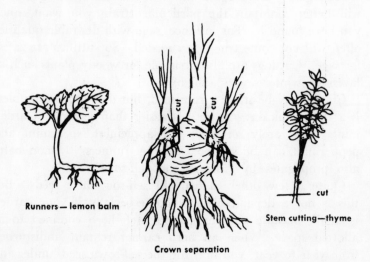

Runners — lemon balm

Crown separation

Stem cutting—thyme

Root Division

Root division is accomplished by dividing one plant into two or more. Tarragon will give you a good example of how you can divide plants by the root method. In the spring choose the plant which you wish to divide. Cut it back to within about 4 or 5 inches from the ground. Next, loosen the soil around the plant, so that you can pull it without breaking the roots which will come apart easily. Plant the new divisions and water them regularly until they are well established. Burn the dead roots which may contain worms or insects.

In dividing woody-stemmed plants such as sage or thyme, cut off a section of the old plant, choosing one to which small roots are already attached. Discard the woody center core and plant the young stems which have several good roots.

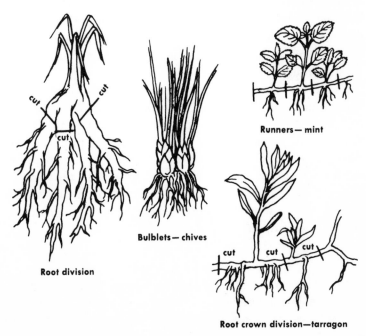

Runners— mint

Bulblets— chives

Root division

Root crown division—tarragon

Stem Cuttings

You probably take stem cuttings often, without thinking of the awkward word "propagating." This process is simply the good old-fashioned custom of taking slips to exchange at garden clubs and over the back fence. Like everything else, there is a right and a wrong way of making cuttings.

Never make a diagonal cut such as you learned to do when arranging flowers. With a sharp knife cut straight across the stem, just below a node, that is, the point at which a leaf is attached. Each section should be from 3 to 6 inches long or a little longer and should have a set of leaves near its upper end. Snip off the larger leaves, leaving only the young leaves and leaf buds on the upper third of the section. Place the cuttings in water as soon as they are removed from the plant. This will prevent wilting.

Next, fill a shallow box, perhaps plastic, with 4 to 5 inches of clean, moist gritty sand or vermiculite. Punch some drainage holes in the bottom of the box. Make a hole in the sand with a pencil or your finger, insert the cutting to a depth of from one-half to two-thirds of its length, pack firmly and wet the sand thoroughly.

Cover the box with either glass or plastic, leaving some ventilation spaces or holes. Put the box in a sunny place and keep moist but not wet, never allowing it to dry out. For the first week or two cuttings should be protected from direct sunlight by paper, cheesecloth or plastic to prevent wilting. On especially hot, sunny days, raise the cover to increase ventilation. Roots should develop in about 2 weeks, and in 4 to 6 weeks the cuttings will be ready to pot, or to put in the garden.

Starting in Water

You can start some cuttings in water. I enjoy a few on the window sill above my kitchen sink where I can watch the baby roots begin to form. If they are near the water

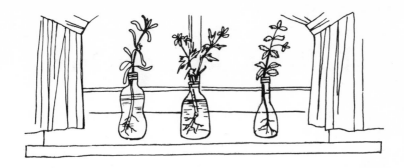

faucet, it is easy for me to remember to keep the bottles filled to the brim. If the roots dry out, even for a short time, the plants may die.

I save attractive bottles, both clear and colored, and they make a pretty row with the green slips of rosemary, mint and rose geranium growing lustily.

Save Your Seed

Since annuals are started each year from seeds, you will want to save some of your own. In this way, you will be assured of getting the variety you want.

Gather the seeds when they are completely ripe. The easiest way is to pick the entire seed umbrels or heads, dropping each variety into a labelled paper bag. In some instances, you may prefer to strip the seeds directly from the plant, especially if you are gathering only a small quantity.

Later you can rub the pods or umbrels between your hands and separate the seeds from the hulls. The safest way of storing is in labelled glass jars, so that they are free from damp and insects.

When you are storing only a few seeds, you can place each variety in a clearly marked envelope and place all of them in a closed jar or can.

6. Hurrah! It's Harvest Time

A great part of the joy of growing your own herbs is in the harvesting. You planted herbs which would produce leaves, flowers, seeds and roots for use during the winter. The great bulk of your harvest will be leaves—parsley and chervil, sage, thyme, basil, marjoram, lemon balm, the savories, tarragon, rosemary and perhaps spearmint.

Of course, you've been using your herbs all summer long. You snipped bits of chives and parsley to scatter over eggs and creamed dishes or to spice up low-calorie diets. You gathered those which took your fancy as you wandered about the garden with the salad bowl in mind, or perhaps tucked a sprig into a favorite book or into your purse for fragrance.

Now it's harvest time, the time when the bulk of your plants must be gathered for your pleasure and use through the winter. Now you can go into the garden and gather reckless loads of fragrance. Harvest time is a time of planning too. You must decide which plants to bring into the house, which to dry, which to make into gifts. You will want to mark those plants which you wish to pot for the winter, even though it is not necessary to dig them until just before frost. When making this decision, keep in mind that you will want:

1. A variety of culinary herbs for the kitchen window sill.

2. A few larger plants to provide sprays for bouquets or iced drinks, to toss into your bath, and for other favorite uses.

3. Several small compact plants to pot for gifts.

4. Pots of plants to place in different rooms throughout your own house.

Just when *is* harvest time? The time for harvesting is decided, not by the time of year, but by the readiness of the herbs. Most herbs are ready to harvest just as the buds are opening into full blossom. This is when the plants contain the most volatile oils and therefore the greatest fragrance and flavor. Fortunately for you, not all varieties will be ready at the same time. But if you should discover that several are just right on the same sunny morning, take a separate box, basket or tray for each herb and label it. Otherwise, unless you are more of an expert than most of us, you may have trouble sorting the herbs after they are dry.

It is best to gather herbs in the early morning of a warm, bright day when the dew has evaporated, but before the sun is high and hot. This is the most pleasant time for being in the garden, and it is a fragrant, relaxing way in which to begin your busy day.

It is important, too, to harvest as early as possible in the season so that the plants will come up again vigorously before the growing season is over. For me, this first harvesting is a difficult decision. I wander about the garden, enjoying the beauty of the plants, their delicious fragrance and lush growth. And each year, in spite of previous years' experience to the contrary, I think, "What if they do not come back again? Will I ruin this lovely garden?"

But don't you believe it! *You are more likely to destroy by holding back than by cutting!* If you wait to harvest perennial herbs late in the season, you will lose not only their flavor but probably the whole plants as well. Do cut early enough to assure regrowth. Otherwise, your plants may die during the winter. Do not cut annuals too close to the ground. Leave enough foliage so that the plants will continue to grow. You may hope for another harvest this season, at which time you can take the whole plant. Cut perennials about two-thirds of the length of the stalks and side branches, less if the stalks are stiff and woody.

You may pick sage, marjoram and basil at any time. The new growth of sage is always flavorful, and so is that of marjoram at any time before the young plants blossom. Basil scarcely has an off-season even though, like other herbs, it is at its best just at blooming time.

If for some reason you do not manage to harvest all you want of a particular herb when it is ready, gather some later on even though its peak cutting season has passed. Once I made a final bottle of basil vinegar in a greedy rush when the weather forecaster said, "Look for a freeze tonight." The resulting product could scarcely be distinguished from that made earlier.

Should the marjoram or thyme that goes into a meat loaf or stew be gathered a bit late in the season, use just a little more and no one except you and a first-rate gourmet will know the difference. However, if the herbs you harvest are to be dried, it *is* important to gather them when the oils are at their best. If you do decide to dry some of the last-minute crops, it might be well to label your jars so that you will know which are prime and which are seconds. Of course, you will also keep some of your favorite herbs growing in the house throughout the winter, and those you will use fresh.

As soon as you have carried your herb crop indoors, quickly rinse off the dirt from the lower leaves and shake off all excess moisture. Then spread the herbs on either window screens laid across two chairs or on some stretched cheesecloth.

Remove any yellowed, decayed and very coarse leaves, and dry your harvest in an airy place away from direct sunlight. For more specific instructions on drying, see Chapter 7.

When to Harvest

Harvest these herbs when they are just starting to bloom:

Basil	Tarragon	Horehound
Mint	Sweet marjoram	Lemon balm
Costmary	Fennel	Winter savory
Sage	Summer savory	Lavender (also may be cut later)

Clip the tops of these at full stage of bloom:

Hyssop   Rosemary

Lavender   Thyme

You can harvest both the leaves and flowers of these four herbs, and you can also pick rosemary leaves separately.

The following herbs should be harvested in the young leafy stage:

Parsley   Caraway leaves

Chervil   Lovage

It is the flower heads of the following herbs that you will want to harvest:

Camomile   German camomile   Marigold

The culinary herbs that you will wish to dry include sweet basil, parsley, thyme, chervil, rosemary, spearmint, marjoram, summer savory, sage, tarragon and lemon balm.

As far as the other culinary herbs in your garden are concerned, do not dry chives, but pot for winter use, put in vinegar or freeze. Dill should not be dried either, but the *leaves* can be frozen fresh or the seeds dried. Parsley may be potted, salted, frozen or dried. Burnet, which is too delicate for drying, can be grown indoors in the winter.

Harvesting Seeds

If you have grown the following plants in your garden, you will want to harvest some seeds for culinary purposes. Use these seeds in and on breads, cookies, cakes, in salad dressings and in countless other ways:

Cumin   Dill   Bene

Burnet   Coriander   Anise

Fennel   Caraway   Clary

Lovage

You should harvest these in the early stages of ripening, just as the seeds turn from green to brown or grey. This will prevent loss by later shattering and will give you a bright, clean product, containing essential oils and tasting its best. Seeds to be garnered for next year's planting should be left on the plants until fully ripe.

Dry seeds thoroughly before storing them. Let them cure for several days in an airy room, then give them a day or two in the sun for extra safety.

7. Preserving and Storing Your Herbs

An herb garden is an easy place in which to practice the "waste not, want not" policy. Every leaf and every flower can go into something, either a vinegar, an herb bouquet, a pomander ball, a collection of teas or dozens of other things. By drying or freezing your herbs you can preserve your entire garden in lovely tastes or scents.

Some herbs take to both drying and freezing, some do not dry well and still others should not be frozen. And it is the leaves of some you will want to preserve, the flowers of others, and in a few cases both leaves and flowers can be used. The following chart will show you at a glance what to do with each of many different herbs.

Herb	Dry	Freeze	Flowers	Leaves
Basil	X	X		X
Burnet		X		X
Camomile	X		X	
Catnip	X			X
Celery tops	X			X
Chervil	X	X		X
Chives		X		X
Costmary	X			X
Fennel		X		X
Lavender	X		X	X
Lemon balm	X	X		X
Lemon verbena	X			X
Lovage	X	X		X
Marigold	X		X	
Marjoram	X	X		X
Mint	X	X		X
Parsley	X	X		X
Pennyroyal	X			X
Rose geranium	X			X

Herb	Dry	Freeze	Flowers	Leaves
Rosemary	X			X
Sage	X			X
Summer savory	X	X		X
Tarragon	X	X		X
Thyme	X	X		X

Dry seeds of:

Anise	Cumin	Lovage
Caraway	Dill	Nasturtium
Coriander	Fennel	Sesame

Drying Herbs

There are several methods of drying which you will enjoy trying, both for variety and to find which is easiest for you.

Rapid Drying

Tender-leafed herbs such as basil, tarragon, costmary, lemon balm and the mints, which have a high moisture content, must be dried rapidly away from the light so that their deep green shade will not fade too badly. The woodier herbs—sage, rosemary, summer savory, thyme—can be partially dried in the sun without being too much affected. Too-long exposure will tend to destroy some of the volatile oils, however, so treat your herbs as tenderly as you do your skin on the first day at the beach.

First, pick off the tops and perfect leaves. Wash if necessary and spread on window screens or frames on which cheesecloth has been stretched. Dry in a room that gets plenty of heat and sun. An attic with a sunny window is ideal, but do not put the herbs directly in the sun. The leaves must be stirred each day for 4 to 5 days. If, instead, you prefer to hang them in small bunches, allow about a week for thorough drying. This method will save you the work of stirring.

Slow Method

In the case of the taller, woodier herbs such as marjoram, sage and savory, you may tie small handfuls loosely together with string and hang, tops down, in a dry place. If grandmother failed to leave you that wonderful house with an attic, the garage or any airy room where you can stretch a line will do. Again, do not dry in the hot sun; I'm repeating, but it's important. You know what the direct sun can do to the oil in your skin. Herbs are tender, too.

When you are sure that the herbs are dry, take them down gently without shaking off the buds of the flowers and store them.

Special Quick Method

Small quantities of parsley, celery tops and mints may be dried by a special quick method. Strip the leaves from the stems, plunge into boiling salted water for half a minute, pat gently between absorbent paper towels or tea towels, and spread the leaves on a fine wire mesh tray or screen in a slow oven just long enough for them to get crisply dry. This takes great care, as I have found from sad experience. Don't answer the phone or doorbell while the herbs are in the oven; don't pick up a book or newspaper "just for a minute." It is wise to prop the oven door open a bit so that the steam will escape. Although this method is adequate if you have no other way of drying, I have found that the resulting flavor is not the best. You can't hurry quality.

Salt Method

An Italian method of preserving basil leaves is to pack them down in a wide-mouthed crock with salt between layers of leaves. When you want to use the leaves, shake off the salt and use the basil as if it were fresh.

Paper Bag Method

If you cannot avoid drying your herbs where dust may

settle—in the garage, for example—you will have to hang the bunches of herbs in paper sacks. Tie the stems into the necks of the sacks, so that they hang free.

No matter what you may have heard, this method is not the best, for proper circulation of air is needed for rapid drying which, in turn, is necessary in order to keep as much as possible of the volatile oils. Still, the sack method is better than not drying the herbs at all, and it has one advantage. When the bags are taken down and before they are untied, you can crush the herbs softly between your hands and store them in less space than would otherwise be required. Should you be forced to use this method, do leave some of the herbs uncrushed, for teas and for foods which call for strong seasoning.

Don't be afraid to try any method which your space and materials make convenient. If you follow the few basic rules of harvesting and drying in this book, you can't go far wrong.

Here, for quick reference, is a summary of herb-drying procedures.

Drying Leaves

Strip leaves from stalk, discarding imperfect and yellowed ones.

Spread in thin layers on clean screen.

Place so air can circulate under as well as over screen.

Gently turn leaves once a day.

Dry for at least 4 or 5 days.

Store in clear glass containers in dark place. Watch a week or longer for signs of moisture.

If moisture forms on the glass, turn the leaves out and dry for a few days longer.

Store in small, opaque containers when perfectly dry. Seal.

Drying Flowers

Cut heads of flowers that are fully opened in the early morning when dew is gone.

Spread petals or florets on a cheesecloth-covered screen, placing them no more than one layer deep.

Put in shady spot where air can circulate well. A warm, airy room is best.

When thoroughly dry, store as leaves.

Drying Seeds

Cut seed heads on a hot, dry day when umbrels are brown.

Gather in large paper bags or in lined baskets. Hold the container under the seed pods or heads as you cut them.

Spread in thin layers on cheesecloth-covered trays or cloth-covered heavy cardboard.

Dry for about one week, occasionally turning or stirring pods.

Rub dry pods through palms of hands. If done out of doors where there is a slight breeze, some of the chaff will blow away.

Spread seeds on screen in a warm, dry spot.

Turn gently once a day for a week or more.

When thoroughly dry, store as you did your leaves, watching for moisture.

Put away in opaque, sealed containers.

Drying Bunches of Herbs

Tie leafy stems in bunches.

Label each variety as it is tied.

Hang bunches on cord strung in airy room, or, if necessary, out of doors in shade. If out of doors, you must bring them in each night.

Dry for about a week until crisply dry. Take bunches down carefully.

Lay each variety on a separate sheet of paper or in a separate basket.

Strip leaves. Wear cotton gloves to protect your hands. Small herbs with tiny leaves and stems need not be stripped.

Flavor is best if leaves are left whole and crumbled as used.

Store as you did leaves.

Storing Dried Herbs

Pack the leaves at once into small jars. Label these and store them in a fairly dark place. Do not be tempted to show off the fruits of your labor in clear glass jars on the window sill, no matter how charmingly old-fashioned and good-housewifely they look. Use pottery or opaque jars with tight covers. If you do use clear glass jars, either paint them black or some other dark shade, or keep them in a dark place. I store my herbs in tin cans or pint jars in a cupboard which is seldom opened. The smaller jars, which are left out for daily use, are refilled from these.

With those herbs which you keep near the stove—and do keep some there along with the salt and pepper—you have an opportunity for attractive display. These are ideally stored in small jars. A collection of very small milk-white cosmetic jars is wonderful. You can label each one with enamel, nail polish, or design your own labels. The smallest available apothecary jars from the variety store are also attractive and inexpensive, and if you like to see herbs through the glass, by all means use these near your stove.

Since these jars are small and you need not fill them to the top, the contents will be used before they lose their fragrance and flavor. Remember—as each jar becomes empty, do not refill on top of the old supply. You will be mixing the fresh with the stale, and the entire jarful will be spoiled. Either use your entire supply before refilling, or in a madly spendthrift way, throw away the last half-inch and replenish from your bank of stored fragrance.

Drying and storing herbs is a bit of work. But when you sprinkle them into the stew pot or brew an aromatic herb tea, you will surely agree with our friend Culpeper: "So shall one handful be worth ten of those you buy."

Freezing Herbs

Some herbs surely must go into your freezer. For one

thing, it is so easy to preserve them by this method that you won't be able to resist. Then, too, there are a few herbs, like dill, chives and burnet, which are not readily adapted to drying.

Even if you potted some of the following herbs so that you could use them fresh, think of the comfort of being able to open the freezer and take out a packet of herbs all ready for the kettle, or to sprinkle over a finished dish. And think of the flavor-insurance should something happen to your growing herbs! Do try freezing a few of these:

Basil	Sorrel	Parsley
Fennel	Chervil	Tarragon
Burnet	Mint	Dill leaves
Lovage	Chives	Sweet marjoram

Now I am not suggesting that you should freeze *all* of your herbs. Some, such as thyme and sage, are not worth the bother. They are as good or better dried. But if you plan to make bouquets of mixed herbs for freezing, you will want to include sage and thyme in the frozen packets.

The method of gathering herbs for freezing is much the same as for those which are to be dried.

Gather in the early morning on a sunny day before the sun is too hot.

Cut tops with stems long enough so that they can be tied in small bunches.

Knot a loop of thread around the stems so that you can dip the herbs into hot water without scalding your fingers.

Arrange sprigs of herbs singly by variety, or in combinations; group them just as you will use them in cooking. Combinations and herb bouquets save time and trouble later, as long as you label them now.

If necessary, wash quickly in cold running water and dry on absorbent paper.

Keep water boiling for blanching. Dip only a few herbs at a time.

Dip completely under the boiling water, immersing the herbs quickly so that they do not become steamed before the water covers them. Keep under water one minute or a little less.

Next, plunge the bundles into ice water for two minutes or hold under running cold water until they are thoroughly chilled.

Drain well.

Place in small freezer bags or wrap in plastic wrapping paper or foil.

Fill small boxes or cartons with the bags.

Label boxes.

Place in the freezer.

Although the blanching-chilling method is generally used for freezing herbs, I have also been successful freezing chives, dill and basil by merely packaging and freezing them fresh from the garden. I chopped up the chives before freezing them by laying the long blades together on a cutting board and slicing them with a sharp knife. Then I sealed them in very small packages of pliofilm in amounts sufficient for single recipes.

You will develop your own preferred methods of packaging and storing. I have a long, rather narrow plastic box which I find very useful. It is divided into sections—but you can make your own dividers of cardboard. In this I store the minced herbs most often used in that form—chives, for example. Write the name of the herb on the divider; a grease pencil is perfect. Lacking that, borrow a crayon from your children. Each packet should contain the right amount to garnish or season a single dish. It is better to keep the packets small, for you can always open an extra if necessary.

Herb bouquets take slightly more storage space than do the individual herbs. You can store a number of the small packets in plastic bags or boxes. Remember to label them! Don't trust your memory as to contents or date frozen. The classic bouquet consists of parsley, bay and thyme sprigs tied together, but on page 115 you will find suggestions for others.

You may also want to freeze "fine herbs" mixtures of four finely minced herbs in different combinations, almost always including chives and parsley or chervil. For recommended fine herb combinations, see page 116.

When using frozen herbs in stews or soups, drop them into the kettle while they are still frozen and tied. If they are to be chopped, they are easier to cut while frozen. Once thawed, use immediately and do not refreeze. You can drop leftovers into vinegars, salads or into salad dressings. Use your frozen herbs just as you would fresh ones.

8. Your Indoor Herb Garden

By now you no longer think of herbs only as bits of dry seasoning, bottled and hidden on the kitchen shelves. There isn't a room in any house or apartment that won't be more attractive with fragrant herbs growing there.

If you are an apartment dweller, surrounded by concrete out of doors, you can have an indoor herb garden. In fact, you can grow almost as many varieties of herbs indoors as you could in an average-sized outdoor garden. On the other hand, if you have an herb garden outdoors, you will enjoy being surrounded by herbs inside too. For example, why not have a sweet scented geranium in your living room? These lovely plants were often found in Victorian parlors. Dittany of Crete (*Origanum dictamus*), immortalized by Virgil, was also popular. Both will fit into your home.

There are several ways to begin your indoor herb garden. You may bring plants in from your outdoor garden, if you have one; start plants from seeds (page 39), from cuttings (page 42) or you may acquire the plants themselves from a friend, a florist or nursery, and then pot them as described later in this chapter.

On page 89 there is a list of herbs that will grow well indoors, with descriptions and instructions for starting them. But here, to give you an idea of the wide choice you have, is a quick rundown.

Herbs to Grow Indoors

Perennials	*Annuals*	*Tender Perennial Shrubs*
Burnet	Anise	Dittany
Chives	Basil	Geranium, scented
Germander	Borage	Lemon verbena
Lemon balm	Chervil	Rosemary
Marjoram, sweet	Dill	
Mint (peppermint and	Lavender	
spearmint)	Parsley	
Sage	Savory, summer	
Tarragon		
Thyme		

The following perennials should be bought as plants, or the plants raised in the garden and brought into the house when they are well established:

Chives	Lemon balm	Lemon verbena	Mint
Rosemary	Sage	Tarragon	Thyme

If you are starting new annuals to bring indoors, plant them late in the season outdoors and transplant before the first frost.

You may plant seeds of sweet marjoram, parsley, basil, dill, anise and coriander directly in your indoor containers. However, I have never had any trouble bringing plants of parsley and basil in from the garden. I choose small plants of basil, since they are apt to grow quite tall, and small parsley plants, since otherwise the taproot would be too deep to transplant.

If you want to grow chives and do not wish to divide your outdoor clump, buy another clump and set it in a bulb pan or low pot filled with light, sweet soil. Cut back the foliage and let new growth start. There is no need to waste the trimmings; chop them and freeze as described in Chapter 7.

Put the chives in a sunny window where they will not get too warm—55° to 60° Fahrenheit is best—and keep them on the dry side. One reason that so many people have trouble keeping chives growing through the winter is the heat of the kitchen.

In your outdoor garden you may have had some perennials such as rose geranium, rosemary and lavender which need the protection of the house during the winter. These plants are not easy to start from seed, nor are the plants themselves readily available. So, once started, you will not want to take the chance of letting them winter-kill. Bring them inside.

If your house space is limited, try this idea. Keep one rose geranium indoors and let it grow as large as it wishes, so that you can cut slips from it. I keep mine in one of the big round planters now so popular. Let the geranium be the focal point of the planter instead of the more usual cut-leaf philodendron, which almost every house plant owner has climbing up a center pole of spagnum moss. Why not be different? Fasten the leggy branches of your rose geranium to the pole, and put your smaller herbs around it. If you want more vividness, tuck in a few artificial flowers. Give the planter a place on the floor or on a low table by a sunny window.

Containers

In general, pots are more successful than boxes for herb growing. Glazed pottery makes good containers since the roots do not dry out as quickly as they will in clay pots. Plastic is satisfactory for the same reason. However, there is one danger with nonporous containers. The plants, if overwatered, may become waterlogged and rot. So if you prefer, you may set unglazed pots in the more decorative containers of glazed pottery or metal.

At a gift shop I saw a large bulb dish holding five tiny pots of herbs. The trouble with the miniature pots is that they will not keep the herbs alive for more than a couple

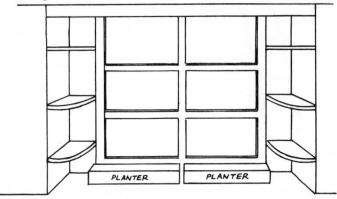

If you are building a new house or remodeling your kitchen, consider a built-in herb garden. A planter at the sink will hold half a dozen herbs, which will thrive happily in sun and moisture. And how convenient for you when you need a bit of seasoning or a sprig for garnishing!

of weeks. With 5-inch pots, you can use your herbs all winter, and set them out again in the spring if you also have an outdoor garden. So, if you use this idea, choose a larger container or fill it with fewer individual pots.

If you do not have enough pots for all your herbs, paint tin cans in bright shades, and letter the names of the herbs in gold or some other paint that contrasts. You may punch a few holes in the sides near the bottom for drainage. Instead of painting, you might prefer to cover the cans with the attractive paper which sticks to any surface and can be kept clean by wiping with a damp cloth.

When you start looking for pots or containers in which to plant your herbs, you will find interesting ideas all around you. Poke into storage shelves, the attic and basement, the kitchen cupboards. A big iron skillet will make an attractive planter when filled with small pots of herbs. First, line it with heavy aluminum foil so that it will not rust, and fill the spaces between the pots with damp peat moss or vermiculite. This suggestion is just to get you started. You will enjoy creating planters or containers out of whatever is handy.

When you are in a remodeling mood, consider a window set at an angle to catch the sun and double the sill planting space.

If you planted a terra cotta jar or strawberry jar for your terrace, it can come indoors for the winter. Some of the plants should be cut back to ensure vigorous growth before frost, while other plants may need to be replaced. Your family room or basement recreation room would be a pleasant place to put the jar. If sun is lacking, consider fluorescent lighting.

Rose geraniums and lemon balm make interesting bathroom decorations. Keep them trim by pinching off fragrant leaves for your bath water.

A small pot of herbs, or a group of several arranged on the dining table, will make a charming scented decoration —and you will enjoy clipping a few leaves to add to salads or drinks.

Potting Soil

Most herbs do best in an alkaline soil. Here is a potting mixture for those which are to be kept indoors:

2 parts good garden loam.
1 part leaf mold or peat moss
1 part sharp sand (not the smooth, fine variety).

To each half-bushel of this mixture add:
1 pint raw crushed limestone or finely crushed plaster
$\frac{1}{2}$ pint bone meal
1 quart well rotted or commercial manure.

Make up the mixture at least two weeks ahead of time so that the soil will have time to become alkalized before you pot the plants.

You may have another potting soil that you prefer, but whatever you use, remember to mix in some limestone. As to the quantity of manure, it is difficult to be exact. Use your judgment, and keep notes for another season. Keep in mind that if you wish to have lush greenery, you should use a rich soil. But for rich flavor and fragrance, use a fairly poor potting soil.

Potting

Drainage is extremely important. If you decide to use nonporous containers start with a few bits of broken clay pot or bits of brick, then add a layer of coarse gravel.

Partially fill the container with potting soil. Set the plant in gently, making a hole in which to lower the root if necessary. Then gently pack more soil about the roots, making sure not to cramp them or to cover the crown, the junction of stem and root. The soil should come to within about one-half inch of the top of the pot. Sprinkle well with water and keep in the shade until the plant sends up leaves.

If you set the pots in saucers, elevate them a bit so that the water can drain out easily.

Artificial Light

If your house or apartment lacks sunlight, consider fluorescent lighting. Artificial light for growing plants is becoming more widely used all the time. You can set up a miniature garden in any corner of your house with the use of fluorescent lighting. A strawberry jar, a china cabinet, a bookcase, a table top or set of special shelves can be made into an indoor garden merely by mounting two 40-watt fluorescent tubes in a fixture over the area. This will be sufficient for a growing area of about 3 x 4 feet, and the tubes should come within a foot of the plants. Keep the lights on for approximately 14 hours a day; the cost will be very little.

If you prefer to use incandescent light bulbs, use 60- or 75-watt bulbs and keep the plants about 2 feet away. This is important since the bulbs give off heat. You will not want to wilt your tender herbs.

Watering

All of your herbs like moisture in the air but not too much in the pots. A weekly watering plus an occasional misting with a fine spray will keep them in good condition.

Water only when the top soil feels dry. Then do not merely sprinkle the top, but wet down thoroughly until you can see water seeping out of the hole in the bottom of the pot. Do not water again until the soil seems dry. Plants may be as easily ruined by too much water as by too little. Keep them damp but not wet.

One of the worst conditions with which house plants must contend is the excessive dryness of the air. A good way to provide the extra moisture they need is to set the pots in shallow trays filled with pebbles. You can use a baking pan, a jelly roll pan or a plastic tray. The heavy aluminum foil pans in which baked goods or frozen foods are packed are excellent for this purpose, and you can find almost any size and shape you need.

If your plants are to be set in the same windows each year, it may pay you to have special trays made to fit the sills. They should be the length and width of the sill and about two inches high. If your window sills are narrow, you can buy or make extensions which can be attached and removed easily.

After these trays or pans are filled with pebbles, add water until it just shows and keep it at that level. Good news: the moisture provided for the plants will be good for your family, too.

Health Hints

Indoor gardening is a healthful hobby. Not only will the herbs stimulate your appetite, but their habits will also help you keep a check on your own. They are fresh-air enthusiasts, and once a day, unless the temperature is far below freezing, open the window and let them breathe. You can breathe right along with them unless you are a softie.

Keep your herbs in a south or southeast window if possible. They are sun worshippers, and the more sun they get, the more they will show their appreciation by vigorous growth. If you don't expect them to do as well indoors as out, you won't be disappointed. We keep our houses much too warm for healthy plants, and unless you have a seldom-used room or a sun porch, you may have to choose between thriving herbs and chilblains.

The temperature which all but the most tender perennials like best is between 50° and 55° F., although some take to warmer rooms. Do not be afraid to try any herb you choose, however. If you turn the heat down at night and keep the plants near a window during the day, they are very likely to survive.

Herbs do not need much fertilizer, but after six weeks you may give them a little balanced plant food once a month if they seem to need it.

Plant lice are not too great a problem with herbs. But if you are moving outdoor plants inside for the winter, it's a good idea to spray them with a soapy solution containing some nicotine insecticide before bringing them into the house. Repeat this at intervals of two or three weeks if you think it necessary.

The automatic pruning as you cut leaves for cookery will keep new foliage coming on, and will encourage a thick and bushy growth. With herbs, you see, you may have your plants and eat them, too!

House-Happy Herbs

Here are some of the herbs which will grow well indoors. Choose as many of these as you can find room for. They will bring fragrance to your home, exciting taste to your foods, and a little fillip to your imagination.

ANISE

Hung over your bed, anise may not make you as fair and youthful as our ancestors believed, but surely the new interest which it brings to foods will keep your appetite young. Although anise is generally grown for its sweet seed, the fresh leaves are appetizing in fruit salads, soups, stews and herb teas.

Start anise from seed or bring in a young plant from the garden and let it have plenty of sunlight.

BASIL

This herb grows particularly well in the kitchen, for it doesn't mind the heat. Keep the plants trim by using the leaves generously in salads, stews, ground meats, poultry stuffings and fruit cups. It is a necessity in any dish containing tomato, or with fresh tomatoes. If you have enough basil, sprays are beautiful in bouquets.

Start basil from seeds or bring in healthy small plants from the garden. You can put three or four light green, smooth-leaved basil plants in the same container. In the spring I set the basil plants back in the garden. These plants can be counted on to produce seed. This is not always true of those raised the first year from seed, because our growing season is too short for seeds to ripen thoroughly.

BORAGE

Although borage is more attractive in the garden than in the house, a pot containing three or four plants will furnish young cucumber-flavored leaves for salads and cool drinks.

If it blooms, the blue flowers are worth the space given this somewhat coarse, hairy-leafed plant. Borage loses its flavor when dried, so use its young, tender leaves.

Start the borage from seed or bring in young plants from the garden.

BURNET

Burnet trails its feathery leaves when grown indoors. It is one of the prettiest plants, and the dainty, cucumber-flavored leaves are delicious in salads. A sprig is attractive in cool drinks.

Because of their trailing stems, burnet, santolina (French lavender), and sweet marjoram are good choices for hanging pots or those placed on shelves at cupboard ends or alongside windows.

Bring burnet in from the garden or buy a plant.

CHERVIL

This fine-leaved herb resembles parsley in looks but not in taste. It is too lovely to look at and too good to eat to be left out of the kitchen herb garden. Bring in a plant and use the fresh anise-flavored leaves for garnishing and to season sauces, soups and salads. The white blossoms are small and fragile. It will germinate rapidly and may be grown from seed.

CHIVES

A clump of chives may be bought at almost any grocery store. If you have both an outdoor and indoor garden, divide a large plant and bring part of it to the kitchen window. The spikey leaves are excellent wherever a delicate onion taste is desired.

DILL

The Orientals used dill in brewing up charms. We "charm" our guests by using its seeds in pickles, fish sauces and salads, but Europeans use the leaves, too, in cooking. Why not try them?

Sow dill seed in a large pot and do not thin it out. It makes a pretty feathery plant. Dill grows rapidly, even indoors, so it may produce its yellow flowers in fairly large umbrels.

GERMANDER

Germander makes a handsome house plant. Its low branching growth is luxuriant with dark green, glossy leaves and small purplish-rose blooms. However, it is not likely to bloom indoors since it needs a great deal of sun if it is to produce flowers. Start germander from seed, cuttings or root division.

LAVENDER

The fragrant lavender makes an especially pleasant house plant. You will have to buy plants to start with. Give them a dry and sunny home. If you have managed to establish lavender in the outdoor garden, it is best to bring the plants indoors for the winter unless you live in a very mild climate.

LEMON BALM

One of the most fragrant of all herbs, lemon balm is worthy of a place in practically any room in the house. Planted outdoors, it grows erect, but when you bring it indoors, the stems tend to trail over the sides of the pot in a lovely effect. Use lemon balm in potpourris, sachets, in the bath water, in floral bouquets, teas, fruit salads and drinks.

If you have lemon balm in the garden, dig up a generous number of plants for the house. Otherwise, get seeds or roots from a nursery.

MARJORAM

Sweet marjoram is one of those herbs which *must* be included in the kitchen window garden. Either dig up a plant, or start a fresh one from seed. Better yet, try both methods. You'll find marjoram well worth the trouble.

MINT

Most popular among the 40 varieties are spearmint and

peppermint. Mint will thrive indoors if kept in a temperature of not more than 65° F. and out of the hot sun. It likes filtered sunlight for part of the day. What a joy to drop a few fresh leaves of mint into a cup of hot tea when you are tired or out of sorts. In winter minced fresh mint in carrots or peas may help you forget that garden-fresh vegetables are still months away.

In the fall pot a clump in heavy soil. Keep it well soaked and let it remain outdoors (on your window sill if necessary) until after the first heavy frost. You can then cut back the tops and bring it inside. Beg a root or cutting from a friend, or buy one at a nursery. The cuttings root rapidly in a glass of water.

Parsley

This herb, one of the oldest known to man, is as popular today as always. When grown in a sunny window in a glazed or metal pot so that the roots will not dry out, it will thrive for a long time. Use rather small plants, for the taproots of mature plants are long. Parsley does better in a cool temperature. Do not use fertilizer. Although parsley will do well inside, it will not be as strong and full as when it grows outdoors. The curly-leafed variety is the prettiest, the flat-leafed type the tastiest.

If you do not have a plant to bring in from the garden, it should be easy to get one from a nursery.

Rose Geranium

Best-known and easiest to find of the fragrant-leaved geraniums is the rose geranium. The leaves are useful in potpourris, sachets and in bouquets, and they are soothing in the tub. A bit of leaf in a cup of tea gives an indescribable fragrance. If you don't know how to use it in apple jelly and cakes, see page 118.

Start new plants with cuttings from an established plant. Since they are sensitive to cold, you must bring rose geraniums indoors in the winter.

Rosemary

Rosemary, the herb of poetry and legend, is not easy to grow, but it is worth the trouble. Grown in a pot as a house plant, it may be less than a foot tall and its lower branches will fall gracefully over the sides of the pot. The leaves resemble long, oval pine needles, particularly when dried. The leaves of rosemary are more fragrant than the flowers, and when gently crushed, they will give off the warm odor of pine.

Rosemary is a tropical plant, and it must be cut back, potted and brought indoors before frost. Your first plant should be purchased from a nursery as it is hard to start rosemary from seed.

Sage

If you can find a small sage bush, it may be brought indoors. Its furry grey-green leaves are attractive and its fragrance pleasant. Although you will probably use sage which you dried during the summer, a growing plant gives a nice variation in hue to your indoor garden.

Tarragon

Tarragon must be brought in for the winter in most climates, and may be set back in the garden in the spring. Early in the summer, start new plants from cuttings, for tarragon does not set seed which will germinate. Plunge the new plants in the earth, pots and all, and let them grow during the summer. When the first heavy frost causes the leaves to fall, you can trim back the stems and transfer the plants to larger pots for wintering indoors. Its young leaves are delicious in eggs, fish, meat and poultry dishes and salads.

Plants must be purchased at a nursery.

Thyme

Thyme will thrive in your window. Use it sparingly, in poultry stuffings, stuffed peppers, onions, zucchini squash, in meat and fish dishes.

Start thyme from seed, and make sure that it has a sunny spot in which to grow.

Part II.
HOW TO USE YOUR HERBS

A Stroll Down Herb Street

You need travel no farther than your herb garden in order to go on a shopping spree. The number of "stores" along the path will surprise and delight you. So put on your gardening hat, slip a basket over your arm, and prepare to spend a pleasant afternoon.

First is the grocer's, offering an endless variety of seasonings to liven up even the plainest dishes. There are herb salts and sugars, herb bouquets to spice your stews, and an amazing number of vinegars: tarragon, burnet, garlic, mint, basil and many more. Then, too, there are the flower vinegars and syrups—rose, carnation, clove-scented pink and others, too.

Difficult as it will be to leave the grocery, you will still hurry on to see what the confectionary has to offer. Do you remember nostalgically the delicately flavored jams, jellies and scented honeys which made a visit to grandmother's such a delight? Well, here they are, waiting for you. You may choose a jelly of thyme or sage or, if you have a sweet tooth, dip into the jar of mint, anise or horehound candies. As a special treat, you may choose candied borage stars, mint leaves, rose petals or violets to charm your guests at your next tea party.

Next to the confectioner's is the pharmacy. If you want

healing lotions, cosmetics or a soothing tisane, they are here. So, too, are perfumes in bottles, and sweet bags, as well as an entire shelf of herbs for the bath. Take your choice. You may wish to relax in the fragrant steam of lemon balm, lavender or rose geranium when you return home.

The bakery will offer you anise cakes and poppy seed rolls, caraway rye bread and rosemary biscuits, along with other mouth-watering choices.

Don't forget to stop at the linen shop. There you will find pillows filled with fragrance. You may choose scented pads to slip among your lingerie, a ribbon sachet to place on the hanger with your smartest dress, or, for the man in your life, select a pine-scented pillow to tuck in his dresser drawer. There are lavender pads to scent the sheets, and pomander balls to spice the coat closet.

Next is the jeweler's where you will see, among other pretty things, a graceful necklace of rose beads smelling of the garden where the roses grew. And there are filigree balls filled with herb and flower mixtures, such as were worn by the ladies of medieval days.

Then the gift shop. Ah, the treasures to be found there! What will you choose? A potpourri for grandmother, a catnip mouse for the kitten, or aromatic tallies for your bridge party? What about a box of hand-decorated notepaper, each sheet with a sprig of rosemary? There is something for everyone here.

No matter how tired you are after your afternoon's shopping, you will want to stop by the florist's. Many flowers are herbs, and he also will have plants and bushes of lavender and rosemary for your own garden. If you are a timid gardener, you may even be able to persuade the florist to start some of the more difficult plants for you. When you leave, take along a quaint tussie-mussie, the small, tight bouquet of fresh herbs and flowers dear to pretty ladies of centuries past.

Ah, here is the tea shop! It is high time for you to rest your aching feet and relax over a cup of hot, aromatic tea. Steaming camomile will give you back your pep. And any other herb tea—catnip, mint, strawberry leaf, orange blossom or others of great variety—will provide a refreshing finish to your afternoon. Perhaps you will also want to order a few lightly buttered wafers topped with fresh leaves of mint, burnet, chopped basil or other fresh herbs.

How Do You Begin?

The amazing variety of seasonings, bath accessories and other interesting things which you saw displayed on Herb Street are all easy to make at home. Surprised? Well, most of them are quite simple, and in the following pages you will find directions for them and many others. Best of all, you need go no further than your own back yard to gather the ingredients.

9. Give and Take From Your Garden

An herb garden is twice blessed, for you can give as much as you receive from it.

Here are some suggestions for using your herbs in many delightful and unusual ways. Remember that many flowers, too, are herbs; so do not be surprised to find roses, violets and other blossoms among the suggested ingredients.

Potted Plants

Remember when you harvested, you marked some of the herbs for potting. Of these, some you planned to keep for your own enjoyment, the others to put back into your herb garden next spring. You probably will want to pot some herbs for gifts. Be as generous as you can, for you will be delighted at the pleasure they will bring. House plants make cherished prizes and imaginative gifts at any time.

A friend in the hospital will enjoy a plant that is not only lovely to look at, but also fragrant to smell and delicious to nibble. Potted herbs are among the best sellers at bazaars and benefits. Get small plastic pots and use some of the smaller plants for this purpose. As the giver you, too, will profit from this project, for you can enjoy the herbs lined up on the window sill as they await gift days.

Bookmarks

Many years ago costmary was known as "Bible leaf" because of the custom of using it as a bookmark in Bibles and prayer books.

Costmary, or any large fragrant leaves such as those of rose geranium, tansy, lemon verbena, or borage, still make charming bookmarks. If, like the women of olden days, you wish them chiefly for fragrance, then press and mount them on cards. Done this way, however, the herbs will soon crumble, so when making bookmarks for gifts, it is better to press them between blotters or tissues between the pages of a heavy book.

When the leaves are dry, place them between two pieces of heavy transparent plastic cut to the size and shape you wish. It is safest to anchor the herb with a bit of glue before putting the second piece of plastic in place. Either seal with glue or punch holes around the edges and lace with yarn

or embroidery floss. I prefer the bookmarks which are laced together, so that some of the fragrance can escape. This is a project which your children will enjoy.

Place Cards and Tallies

For a dinner, luncheon or card party you can make attractive place cards and tallies decorated with herbs. Cut plain cards twice the size you wish them to be when finished and fold in the center. On the outside cut a slit and insert a sprig of fresh or dried herb; you can attach the spray to the card with transparent tape of you prefer.

You can make a place card which doubles as a favor by attaching a sachet to a card. For benefits or bazaars, package these in sets of eight or twelve.

Herb Bouquets

A quaint name for these bouquets is "tussie-mussies." For centuries they have been carried by those participating in the coronation ceremonies in England. Elizabeth II was handed a tussie-mussie as she entered Westminster Abbey. Long ago they were no doubt carried to ward off germs and to counteract unpleasant smells resulting from lack of adequate ventilation and plumbing. Today, however, tussie-mussies are valued for the sentiment of the meaning attached to the various herbs and for their charm in appearance and fragrance.

In the 15th century a favorite tussie-mussie was made of marigold (for happiness) and heartsease (for remembrance). Others were often used also. For example:

A red rosebud surrounded by forget-me-nots and southernwood signified undying devotion, remembrance and constancy.

A spray of bee balm, southernwood and Bible leaf (costmary) was tucked into the bodice of the Sabbath gown to be sniffed during the long Sunday church service.

Sage with white and gold camomile flowers symbolized long life, wisdom and patience.

Lavender was thought to bring the wearer luck, and heartsease and lily of the valley surrounded by marjoram signified humility, purity and happiness.

These are only a few of the meanings associated with various herbs. When you present a tussie-mussie, write on your card the significance of the bouquet which you have assembled. Although 15th-century belles knew the meaning of each herb, the girls of today are likely to confuse the sincerity denoted by foxglove with the flattery of fennel.

Make a tussie-mussie for a sick friend; use them as place cards; or take them to a hospital ward or an old people's home.

To make the bouquets, choose small roses, forget-me-nots, clove pinks or violets—any small, delicate flowers. Around the center flower, group fragrant herbs such as sprigs of lavender, lemon verbena, rosemary, sweet-scented geranium, lemon balm or other sweet-smelling leaves. Basil, bergamot, marjoram or any of the mints are also good.

Cover the stems with a bit of dampened cotton, then with aluminum foil. Surround with a paper doily or stiffened lace, and tie with a ribbon.

Seed Packets

Package small envelopes of seeds. On each one letter the name of the herb or, better still, paste its picture on the appropriate envelope. With the mounting popularity of herbs, you will not find it difficult to get pictures.

You may want to tie an assortment of seed packets into a package. The gift will be even more appreciated if you include directions for planting the seeds.

Corsages

Make five-petaled flowers, perhaps wild roses, out of nylon, organdy or any other pretty, fairly thin but nonporous cloth. Each petal should be made double, like a tiny envelope, and filled with dried rose petals and herbs or with one of the rose jar mixtures described later in this chapter. Sew the petals together in the form of a flower and add a couple of artificial leaves. These fragrant corsages will not only be good money raisers for your church or for other organizations, but will also make lovely place cards. Hospital patients especially enjoy them.

Pomander Balls

One of my less happy school memories is of having to stand beside a child who wore an asafetida bag. It was supposed to ward off disease—and perhaps it did. Certainly this child was not likely to come into close contact with those who had a contagious germ!

In ancient times, when sanitary measures were practically unknown, physicians advocated the use of herbs to protect not only individuals but whole communities as well. Had I known of the medicinal properties of rue, rosemary and bay in my early school days, how I would have longed to substitute a pomander ball for the satin bag of my schoolmate.

Ancient pomander balls were elaborate and expensive, but the common people could and did substitute wax balls impregnated with herbs, or even carried bunches of herbs with them wherever they went.

The pomander balls which we know today are not worn as were those of olden days, and are much less expensive, being made with a foundation of fruit rather than enclosed in a silver or gold filigree sphere.

Children love making pomander balls, and many clubs and community groups have used them to raise funds. However, you must start this project at least six weeks before you want to use the completed balls.

Start with an orange, an apple, a lime or lemon. With apples especially, be sure that the fruit is firm and free from blemishes. Stick the fruit full of whole cloves, placing them in rows that touch one another. When we made them in our community, the girls wore thimbles, but the boys stuck up their noses at such a feminine accessory. One of them came up with the idea of cutting a finger from an old leather driving glove or canvas gardening glove; this worked admirably to protect tender finger tips.

When the fruit is completely covered with cloves, put it in a cool, dry place for a month or more. After it has dried out, make a mixture of orrisroot and an equal amount of spices and herbs—cloves, nutmeg, cinnamon, allspice, rosemary, rose geranium, or any fragrant substance you choose. If you use several varieties of fruit, you might like to vary them by using ground cinnamon for the spice on the apples, nutmeg on the limes, and cloves for the lemons. Blend the herbs and spices well. Do not omit the orrisroot, whatever else you use, for it is the fixative which holds the other ingredients together.

Roll the fruit in the orris-spice mixture until it is thoroughly coated. Leave it in the box with the powder for one to two weeks. After this final storage period, shake off the powder and tie each piece of fruit with ribbon, crossing it so that the ball is divided into fourths. Make a loop at the top so that the pomander can be hung in the clothes or linen closet.

If you prefer, you can wrap the balls in squares of nylon net, gather it in at the top with a ribbon and sew on the bow so that the pomander may be hung by one of the loops.

Kittens' Delight

Cat owners will gratefully accept gifts for their pets, or troop to a booth at a bazaar when you sell catnip bags and cushions. Have the artist of your group draw a simple outline of a mouse, or trace one from a nursery rhyme book. Sew two of these outlines together, leaving a small opening, fill with dried

catnip and sew up the remaining opening. If this involves too much work, you can make small squares or rectangles and outline a mouse with embroidery floss or textile paint. I don't suppose that a cat will object to an undecorated bag, but her mistress will be more likely to buy a fancier one.

For the pillows, which bring a good price, mix a goodly amount of catnip in with whatever filling you use.

Sweet Bags or Sachets

An old-fashioned custom which you may want to revive is that of making sweet bags to hang on the backs of upholstered chairs, place in dresser drawers, linen and clothes closets, under pillows and in chests.

Make the bags of silk, organdy, nylon, or any other pretty fabric and leave a ribbon loop so that they can be hung in closets or pinned to curtains or chairs. They may be any shape you wish, as simple or as elaborate as your fancy and ability direct. If you are of the minimum-work school, you can use small chiffon handkerchiefs or squares of chiffon, silk or organdy. Put a handful of dried flowers or herbs in the center, tie with a pretty ribbon and there you are—you don't even have to know how to sew to make a lovely sachet.

Here are some especially fragrant sachet mixtures:

Lavender flowers, rose geranium leaves, roses, lemon verbena.
Any fragrant leaved geranium with rosemary.
Equal parts of peppermint, lemon verbena, lemon balm, rose geranium and rose petals.
Lemon thyme with verbena.
Costmary and fragrant-leaved geranium.
Lavender, rosemary, a few cloves and a bit of lemon or orange zest. (Zest is the outer layer of citrus fruit, with no white attached, pared from the fruit and dried.)

Experiment with mixtures. Add spices—ground cloves, cinnamon, allspice, ginger—alone or in combinations to the flowers and herbs. A few crushed anise or coriander seeds give an elusive fragrance.

Here are a few mixtures which are particularly nice for the linen closet:

4 parts lavender, 2 parts rose petals, 1 part southernwood.
3 parts lavender, 1 part bergamot, 1 part lemon balm.
Equal parts of sweet fern, bergamot, lemon balm.
Equal parts of rose geranium leaves, lemon thyme and lemon verbena.

For the clothes closet, pomander balls are nice, as are padded clothes hangers filled with sachet mixtures. Or you may want to make small bags to place on each hanger. A fragrant mix is made of:

2 parts rose petals, 1 part rose geranium, 2 parts lavender,
1 part thyme.

Don't neglect the men. Whether or not they will admit it, they, too, like a bit of not-too-sweet fragrance. Sniff their hair oils and shaving lotions if you don't believe me. For men, make sachets containing one of the following blends and slip a bag into your husband's dresser drawer or hang it in his clothes closet.

Equal parts of:
Pine and lavender.
Lavender, verbena, nutmeg and geranium.
Lemon balm, thyme and lavender.

A tablespoon of mixed spices may be added to each quart of any of the above mixtures.

Drawer Pillows

These are lovely gifts for anyone, including yourself. Make flat "pillows" of any thin but nonporous material. A bride would be thrilled to receive several in her favorite shades: pink for her lingerie drawer, green for the handkerchief box, mauve for the linen closet. Fill these pillows with rose petals, lavender, carnation petals, or a mixture of rose geranium and lemon verbena. Costmary with rose geranium is another good mixture.

It is wise to quilt or tie the pads in several places. You may prefer to place the scented leaves between thin layers of cotton or cheesecloth before adding the fancy outer fabric.

For the Linen Closet

Scented flat pads are wonderful to put between piles of linens. Make them about 7 x 9 inches in size, fill them with enough mix to make a rather plump pad and tuft in several places. You will need to crush or shake the pads every week or so to release their fresh fragrance.

Godey's Lady's Book in 1864 gave these directions for a mixture to keep away moths: Cloves, in coarse powder, one ounce; cassia, one ounce; lavender flowers, one ounce; lemon peel, one ounce. Mix and put into little bags; place them where the clothes are kept.

Listed among the old-fashioned moth preventatives were lavender, peppermint, rosemary, spearmint, tansy, sweet woodruff, any or all blended with spices.

How much more pleasant these fragrances than the over-powering odor of moth balls.

Herb Pillows

In Biblical days, women filled pillows with mandrake to keep evil spirits from harming the family while they slept. You may make pillows of any pretty cotton or silk, cut so they will be about 4 x 6 inches when finished. Fill them with any sachet mixture of your choice.

You can make an especially soothing mixture from equal parts of rosemary blossoms, rosemary leaves and pine needles, dried thoroughly and slightly crushed.

Rose geranium and lemon verbena or lemon balm also combine well with pine needles.

When you have worked your way up to more elaborate mixtures, try this one:

2 tablespoons whole cloves (crushed)	1 tablespoon allspice
2 sticks cinnamon	1 teaspoon cardamon seed
1 teaspoon caraway seed	½ dried rind of a medium orange

In a separate bowl, mix 1 cup each of dried rose geranium leaves, lavender flowers, lemon thyme and rosemary; 2 cups sweet marjoram; 1/2 cup spearmint and lemon or orange mint, mixed.

Fixative: 2 tablespoons crushed orrisroot, 2 tablespoons gum benzoin, 10 drops bergamot oil.

Make a layer of herbs, sprinkle with spices, then fixatives. Repeat until all ingredients are used. Let stand in airtight containers about two months. Use to fill small bags to put under pillows.

If it tires you even to think of all this work, don't give up. You can make nice pillows of rose petals, lavender or pine needles alone.

The Scented Bath

Children and adults alike enjoy a scented bath, so here is another homemade gift with a professional look and an elegant fragrance.

Dry large quantities of lemon balm, lemon verbena, sweet marjoram, rosemary, bergamot or other mints, lavender and rose geranium, or any other fragrant leaves. After they are dry, put these leaves in pretty glass jars. You can either make a mixture of fragrances, or put each one in a separate jar.

When bathing, first steep about half a cupful—more, if you are a deep-water addict as I am—in boiling water for about 15 minutes. Strain into the bath water. Now you can lie back and relax in luxury.

Bath bags are wonderful gifts. Make cheesecloth bags which will hold a handful of dried herbs. Fill them with individual leaves or blends as you choose. Pack the bags in a pretty glass jar. Remember to label it. You won't want these sweet herbs to land in your friend's stew pot!

Potpourris and Rose Jars

Long before the days of Nero, and up to the 20th century, so little was known of ventilation and sanitation that the practice of strewing herbs indoors was a necessity. The only known way of getting rid of filth was to cover it with a layer of fresh straw and herbs. In medieval days, rue, hyssop and other herbs were scattered over floors of castles and cottages. Sweet woodruff, rosemary and lavender were strewn in the bedchamber. And up to the last century rue was strewn in the chambers of English judges to get rid of evil odors and vermin.

We now have more pleasant reasons for using herbs, and the potpourri spreads its fragrance in our clean, airy rooms even more happily than it did in great-grandmother's stuffy parlor.

Here are some favorite potpourris from long, long ago.

Potpourri

1 quart dried rose petals	1 cup dried rosemary
1 pint dried rose geranium leaves	2 tablespoons each crushed whole cloves, cinnamon, allspice
1 pint dried lavender flowers	

Fixative: 3 tablespoons each, crushed orrisroot and gum benzoin.

> 20 drops rose oil compound
> 5 drops heliotrope oil compound
> (You can get these oils at the pharmacy.)

Store the potpourri in a tight container for 2 months.

Rainbow Potpourri

Take choicest petals of pink, red and yellow roses, lavender blossoms, petals of pink and blue delphiniums, larkspur, cornflower, yellow and orange calendulas, purple sweet violets and pansy heads. Add scented geranium and lemon verbena leaves. To each gallon of dry blossoms and leaves add 1 heaping tablespoon of a fixative such as powdered orris. To the fixative add 1 tablespoon mixed powdered spices—cloves, allspice and nutmeg, with enough essential oil to form a loose mixture. Mix with petals and leaves and let stand 6 to 8 weeks.

(Essential oils—rose, garden bouquet, Persian garden— can be bought from wholesale distributors or in some pharmacies.)

If you would like a jar containing roses only, you will find this a quick and easy recipe:

Dry rose petals in the usual way (page 74) and pack firmly in a jar, spreading each one-inch layer with salt. Tamp down as additional petals are added.

When thoroughly dry, add the following mixture to one quart of leaves:

1 ounce each, ground	½ ounce anise seed
cinnamon, nutmeg, cloves	2 ounces powdered orrisroot
1 ounce sliced gingerroot	

Mix with the petals and keep in a covered jar.

There are many recipes for potpourri, but there are only two methods of preparing it. The *moist* method was the old-fashioned custom of first partially drying the flowers and herbs, then adding salt, and finally the other ingredients. This gives a stronger odor than does the alternate method, but it causes the color to be lost. You will have to choose between the two, or perhaps you'll decide to make a little of both.

The *dry* method calls for drying the petals thoroughly and then mixing in sweet-smelling leaves and petals along with spices and orrisroot. In this way you can preserve much of the original color of the petals.

Whichever method you choose, gather petals of full-blown, fragrant flowers early in the morning. Dry them as you do your culinary herbs. You can use a window screen placed on two chairs, or if you have a curtain stretcher or quilting frame stowed away in the attic, cover it with cheesecloth and bring it back into use. Do your drying in a warm, dry place and stir the petals often.

Moist Method

Dry the petals for a couple of days until they are leathery but not dry enough to crumble. Put in a wide-mouthed jar with a tightly fitting cover. Choose one large enough so that it will be only about two-thirds full when all of the petals have been put inside.

Put half an inch of flowers in the jar, cover with a sprinkling of uniodized salt mixed with coarse salt (using about one-third salt to two-thirds petals). Each day as you gather petals, dry them. Then thoroughly stir those already in the jar, and add the new layer of flowers and salt.

If you have an old-fashioned wooden potato masher, it is perfect for the next step. Press down the flowers and salt and put a weight on top—don't use metal. A small saucer weighted with a rock, such as your grandmother used in making dill pickles or kraut, is fine.

The weight will press juice from the petals and as the fluid rises, stir it thoroughly. When the action has stopped, leave the jar alone for about 10 days. You will then find that a rather hard mass has formed. Break this mass into bits and mix with spices or oils and the fixative. Now, let it stand in a tightly covered jar for about 6 weeks.

One ounce of fixative to 2 quarts of petals is a good proportion. Probably you will choose orrisroot as the fixative.

As for spices, try equal proportions of crushed nutmeg, cloves, cinnamon, mace and allspice—about a heaping tablespoon to each quart of petals. You may add a few drops of essential oils—bergamot, rose, geranium, bitter almond, orange flower, rosemary—but do not use too many kinds. Start slowly, and add more scents as your sniffing dictates.

Of course the individual spices and oils which you use will vary according to your tastes. After you have tried several mixes, you will discover the fragrance which exactly pleases you.

Dry Method

The dry method is much simpler than the moist, and you are more likely to choose it. This is especially true if you wish to make potpourri in large quantities, either for sale or for gifts.

Dry your roses, petals and buds of the most fragrant varieties, in a dry, airy room out of the sun. Sprinkle with a light layer of uniodized salt. Then add dried herbs and other flowers of your choice. You may use some flowers for vividness only with the fragrant varieties. Blue borage stars, yellow calendula, bachelor buttons or other bright, small whole flowers are pretty. All herbs and flowers must be thoroughly dried before you add them to the roses. The rose petals must predominate. As you add flowers and leaves, also add more salt.

For fragrances other than that of the rose, you may choose pinks, carnations, mignonette, orange blossoms, syringia or any other flowers you like. Marjoram, anise, basil, and perhaps a bit of cedar may go in the jar, too. Avoid herbs of extremely strong fragrance, such as pennyroyal and mint.

When the mixture is well dried, add one-fourth ounce each of powdered cloves, mace and cinnamon and one-eighth ounce crushed coriander, cardamon seed and powdered gum benzoin and gum storax. Mix well again and, if you wish, add a drop of attar of roses and an ounce of violet sachet. Leave the potpourri tightly closed in a jar for at least a month.

Whichever method you use, you are now ready to choose your containers. Any pretty jar will do, whether it is an antique rose jar or a variety-store glass container. Each day as you lift the cover, your garden will come wafting up to you.

10. Having Your Herbs and Eating Them Too

Vinegars

Do you know that there are more than sixty varieties of vinegar? And how many do you use? Cider, tarragon, perhaps one or two more—and you with your herb garden! It's time that you put more of those taste-teasers to use. You will never again use plain vinegar once you have become acquainted with those flavored with herbs.

Especially good for culinary purposes are vinegars made with burnet, basil, dill, thyme, the mints and chives. Delightful vinegars may also be made with rosemary, caraway, fennel, garlic, marjoram, rose geranium, borage and sorrel. In days gone by, vinegars were also made with flowers. They are still worth adding to your collection, and you may choose from rose, clove pink, carnation, elder blossom, rosemary, gilly flowers, and other spicy scented blossoms.

Vinegars provide the easiest possible way in which to get herb fragrance into your salads; they make wonderful gifts; they are easy to store and use. And I know of no better therapy for tired minds and nerves than that of gathering the ingredients and making the vinegars.

There are several ways of making herb vinegars, but to me the one I am about to describe is the most simple as well as the most enchanting.

You need not be as particular about the time of harvesting herbs to make your vinegar as when you are gathering herbs to dry. In the early morning I take a half-pint jar into the garden. If I plan to make more than one vinegar that day, then of course I take a jar for each herb. In the jar I pack the leafy tips and young leaves of whatever herb I have chosen. When the jar is two-thirds full, into the kitchen I go.

Although wine vinegar is best, you can use any good white or red vinegar as a base. Heat it until it is just warm, not hot, and pour it over the herbs. It is best to cover the jar with aluminum foil or waxed paper before putting on the lid; as you probably know, vinegar will rust metal. If you are fortunate enough to have some glass-topped jars, use them.

Some people keep the jars in the sun; others favor a cool, shady place. Not having a sunny window available, I simply keep them on the kitchen counter near my sink where I am reminded to shake them at least once a day. After about two weeks, you should taste the vinegar for flavor. A few drops are sufficient for seasoning, as the flavor becomes quite strong.

You will have a choice as to methods of bottling. I put aside a pint jar with leaves and vinegar and use it just as it is. This conserves space, and besides, I like to see the leaves of the herbs. The remainder of the vinegar I strain through a muslin cloth or a double layer of cheesecloth, and then bottle it. For gifts, I have found a nail polish remover bottle of interesting design and of just the right size. I save these, and fill them as needed with the filtered vinegar. I fill some while the herbs are still fresh in the garden, and I push a spray of the appropriate herb into the bottle where it stays suspended.

Although we prefer most vinegars warmed before being poured over the herbs, here are some exceptions:

Dill Vinegar

½ cup dill leaves

1 pint mild white vinegar

1 tablespoon chervil if available

Pour hot vinegar over leaves. Let stand in sun 3 to 4 weeks, shaking occasionally. Strain before bottling.

Mint Vinegar

1 quart white vinegar
2 cups spearmint leaves
1 cup sugar

Boil 5 minutes, crushing mint. Strain and bottle hot. Use in iced tea or punches. A bit of mint vinegar brushed over lamb while roasting adds a subtle tang.

Elder Flower Vinegar

Gather elder flowers on a sunny day. Pluck them from their stalks and dry quickly and thoroughly on trays above the stove or in oven with door open. Pack in quart jars. If you wish to be precise, allow one pound of flowers to each pint of vinegar. White wine is the best for this variety. Heat vinegar to boiling point and pour over the flowers. (For vinegars made of fresh flowers, vinegar only warmed is better, but the hotter liquid helps distill the flavor from dried flowers.) Cover jars tightly and keep in a warm place for 8 to 9 days, shaking occasionally. Strain, bottle and seal. This is especially good with fruit salads such as pear or apple.

If you would like a more complicated recipe, try this:

Herb and Spice Vinegar Française

$\frac{1}{4}$ ounce each dried, or 1 tablespoon fresh leaves of basil, rosemary, mint and tarragon
$\frac{1}{2}$ ounce dried, or 2 tablespoons fresh marjoram
4 crushed bay leaves
1 teaspoon dill seed, crushed
$\frac{1}{4}$ teaspoon whole cloves, crushed
$\frac{1}{2}$ teaspoon black pepper
$\frac{1}{4}$ tea-spoon allspice
2 quarts red wine vinegar (or cider vinegar)

Blend herbs and spices in a wide-mouthed jar. Pour vinegar over them. Let stand in warm room for 2 or 3 weeks, stirring occasionally. Strain through filter paper or fine cloth. Pour in bottles and cork tightly. Use 1 teaspoon to 1 tablespoon in meat and steak sauces, stews and ragouts.

Here, again, you can have the fun of experimenting. Let

yourself go wild with combinations of flavors, all dropped into the same small bottle of vinegar or dressing. One day when you taste it, it will be perfect. Use it with joy, for you will not be able to duplicate your "hit and miss" recipe, but don't let that bother you; your next bottle of catch-all may turn out to be superb.

Just to get you started, here are a few ways in which you can add excitement to your menus with herb vinegars:

Tarragon: Use a bit in Harvard beets, for marinating chicken before baking, or in fish marinade.

Mint: ½ teaspoon in peas and green beans with ½ teaspoon sugar (for 4); 2 or 3 teaspoons on roast lamb.

Basil: In soup, hot beets, hot greens, cauliflower, Brussels sprouts, broccoli and salads.

Marjoram: In salads, especially asparagus.

Garlic: In baked beans, apple salad, chicken and soup.

Herb Mixtures

In herb cookery you will often hear the phrases "herb bouquet" and "fine herbs."

Herb bouquet: Three or four fresh herbs tied together. The bouquet is removed after cooking. The classic combination consists of parsley, celery leaves, onion and a sprig of thyme, but there are many variations.

A simple bouquet consists of 3 sprigs of parsley, a bay leaf and several blades of chives. For a slightly more elaborate mixture, package together celery leaves, chervil, sage, marjoram and chives. Thyme, basil, summer savory and chives make

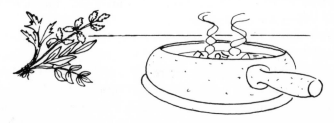

a popular combination, as do basil, thyme, parsley and marjoram. Much of the fun comes with experimenting and developing your own favorites. Here are a few additional combinations:

For stews: parsley, thyme, clove
    or
    rosemary, parsley, celery
    or
    sweet marjoram, parsley, onion
For ragout of beef: burnet, chervil, chives, tarragon
For soup: rosemary, celery, parsley, basil, savory or thyme
For tomato soup: basil, parsley, onion, bay leaf

Fine herbs: This is a finely minced mixture of 4 or 5 herbs in different combinations, but always including chives and either parsley or chervil.

Here are 4 combinations. Start each with chives and parsley or chervil.

Add: burnet, tarragon, basil, thyme
    or
    burnet, tarragon, marjoram
    or
    savory, burnet

With dried herbs, use smaller quantities; approximately 1 tablespoon fresh equals 1 teaspoon dried.

Usually fine herb combinations are tied up in cheesecloth and removed before the food is served.

There are herb mixtures in endless variety, and perhaps you will wish to make your own combinations. But here are some which have proved good.

For ground beef: 1 tablespoon dried basil, celery, parsley, savory, marjoram, thyme. Use 1 teaspoon for each pound in meat loaf containing crumbs or any other "stretcher," ½ teaspoon for each pound of ground beef for hamburgers.

For tomato juice: 3 teaspoons basil, 1 teaspoon each, celery leaves, thyme, parsley, crumbled bay leaf. Make into soup bags by putting 1 heaping teaspoon and a whole clove in a 4-inch square of cheesecloth and tying with a string. Keep bags in an airtight container. Use 1 bag to 2 quarts tomatoes.

Herb mixtures make the nicest of gifts for those who enjoy cooking, and they sell well at bazaars. Whether made up for gifts, for sale or for your own use, do not neglect careful labelling, or else the right herbs may go into the wrong pot. You might make up several different mixtures, label them and package three kinds in a jar.

"For Meats" could contain rosemary, parsley, bay, lemon zest, whole cloves and peppercorns.

"For Fish" might include basil, parsley, thyme, bay, lemon zest, peppercorns and, if available, fennel or fennel seed.

"For Poultry" could include savory, thyme, marjoram, parsley and bay, with perhaps some of the convenient instant onion flavorings now on the market.

Herb Salts

If you are in the habit of using only onion- and celery-flavored salts, add some of your own herb salts to your spice chest.

Mix 1 cup of salt (not iodized) with $1\frac{1}{2}$ cups minced fresh herbs, either a single variety or a combination of several. If you have an electric blender, whirl for about 3 minutes. Otherwise, mix thoroughly by hand. Spread in a thin layer on a cooky sheet or aluminum foil tray and dry in a very slow oven—150° or even lower. Keep the door open a bit.

Herb Sugars

You can make delightful flavored sugars by putting a few leaves of rose geranium, lemon mint, spearmint or lemon verbena in a jar of sugar. Leave it for a week or two, stirring occasionally. Sift out the leaves and bottle for use in cakes or puddings, on sugar cookies or cakes. You may color the sugars if you wish: yellow for lemon mint, green for spearmint, rose for geranium. You can use fragrant violets or rose petals in the same way.

Sweets from the Herb Patch

Don't forget about herb jellies. Tarragon, basil, rosemary and lemon verbena make especially good ones. Although rose, violet and marigold jellies are expensive luxury gifts, you can make them simply and inexpensively in your own kitchen. Some mixtures that are very pleasing are:

Sage and cider   Thyme and grape
Marjoram and lemon   Savory and grapefruit
Mint and honey   Rose geranium and orange

Thyme Jelly

1 cup herb infusion   ½ bottle pectin
¼ cup vinegar   3 cups sugar

For infusion, pour 1¼ cups boiling water over 2 tablespoons thyme. Cover. Let stand 15 minutes. Add water if needed to make 1 cup after straining into a 3-quart pan. Now, proceed according to the directions on the pectin bottle.

Serve jelly on roast chicken.

Apple Jelly as a Base

You can make herb jellies from angelica, apple mint, basil, costmary, lavender, lemon verbena, spearmint, rose geranium (especially delicious on hot breads), rose petals and many other flowers and leaves. Just place the herbs in the bottom of the glass and pour in the apple jelly.

Sage Jelly

Pour 1½ cups boiling water over ¼ cup dried sage. Cover. Let stand for half an hour. Strain. Add water to make 1 cup liquid. Add ¼ cup vinegar, 1 tablespoon lemon juice and 3 cups sugar.

Place over hottest heat and stir until a full rolling boil is reached. Add ½ bottle pectin. Boil for half a minute. Skim and pour. Makes three 6-ounce glasses.

Serve with poultry and pork.

Basil Jelly

4 cups apple juice   2 tablespoons lemon juice
2 cups sugar   12-14 sprigs fresh basil

Boil juices, stirring until sugar is dissolved. Add basil and boil to jelly stage. Strain into jelly glasses. When cool but not set, put 3 or 4 basil leaves in each glass. Seal. Makes 4 to 6 small glasses.

Canned Peaches or Pears

Put a bunch of sweet herbs such as lemon geranium, lemon verbena, lemon balm, mint, or rose geranium in the boiling syrup and let it soak. Remove before pouring the syrup over the fruit in the jars. Don't go overboard. Start with small amounts, adding more herbs as desired.

Rose Petal Jam

Use the petals of red, fragrant roses. For 50 full-blown roses allow 2 pints of water and 3 pounds of sugar. Boil the sugar and water until it is slightly thick. Add the juice of a small lemon and the rose petals. Simmer for an hour, stirring very frequently so that it will remain red. Pour into tiny pots and cover when cold.

Candied Borage Stars

Pick the blue flowers when they have fully opened. Brush with egg white beaten just enough so that it can be applied easily; use a small paint brush. Dust with sifted granulated sugar and spread on waxed paper to dry in a cool place.

Mint leaves, rose petals and violets may be candied in the same way.

Store these sweets in airtight cans with waxed paper between the layers. They also freeze well.

Tisanes

In centuries past, herb teas were called "tisanes," and were drunk just before bedtime to soothe the nerves and induce restful sleep. Herb teas were also used because they were economical and for their medicinal value. Some favorites were:

Sweet marjoram with a little mint
Thyme with a little hyssop
Sage with balm leaves to which was added lemon juice
Rosemary with lavender flowers
Clover and camomile

120

Leaves of a red rose and sweet myrtle
Strawberry leaves and the leaves of sweetbriar
Goldenrod and betony with honey
Peppermint and yarrow

A good imitation of a China tea is made of a mixture of dried strawberry, raspberry or blackberry leaves with an equal amount of peppermint and thyme or lemon thyme. If you wish, you may add elder or orange or lavender blossoms.

You can use herbs either fresh or dried, singly or in combinations. Some are bitter, some sweet. Our ancestors chose "a tonic dose of bitters" for their health. Especially esteemed for their medicinal and tonic virtues were:

Mint	Catnip	Lavender flowers	Wormwood
Basil	Bergamot	Fraxinella	Thyme
Tansy	Rosemary	Feverfew	Camomile
Yerba-buena	Costmary	Pennyroyal	flowers
Lemon balm	Horehound	Fennel	German,
Verbena	Sage	Southernwood	not the
			common
			variety

Even today an exclusive beauty salon serves expensive cups of camomile tea with cream and sugar. They are wrong in a way—cream or milk should never be used with herb teas. But the use of camomile tea is the same as in the middle ages when it was quaffed to soothe the nerves of the court beauties. Perhaps we should go back to herb teas instead of using the controversial modern tranquilizers.

To make camomile tea, dry the flower heads as they come into bloom. This is one herb in which the flower heads contain the oil. Pour 1 quart of boiling water on less than ½ ounce of dried flowers. Let stand 15 minutes. Strain. Sweeten with honey or sugar. Take at bedtime for quiet sleep.

The French in particular drank tisanes as nightcaps. They were fond of camomile, lemon balm, orange blossom and linden. These are at their most delicious when sweetened with honey. Also popular were teas of strawberry, blackberry or raspberry leaves, sage and anise. The dried leaves, bark, roots and flowers of at least 50 herbs, shrubs and trees were used to make aromatic drinks.

A cup of tea is restful, and when you become tired while working in the garden, what could be more refreshing than to brew a cup of herb tea? Pick a generous tablespoon of the leaves of lemon balm, peppermint, spearmint, rosemary or

anise. If a dried herb is used, add only 1 teaspoon of leaves or flowers to a cup of water. Pour a cup of boiling water and let steep 5 minutes. Drink plain or with a slice of lemon. If you wish, you may sweeten with honey or sugar. Drink slowly and happily. Relax, so you will go back to your garden well refreshed.

You can prepare tisanes at any time of the year from dried herbs, just as was done hundreds of years ago. But remember that 1 tablespoon of chopped fresh herbs equals ½ tablespoon of the dried. Some teas must be boiled; others require steeping only as do the usual teas we all buy. Catnip,

marjoram, sage, camomile and the mint teas should be steeped. Put a handful of the leaves in a pottery or glass pot, pour over them a pint of boiling water and steep for ten minutes. Although sweetening was not used in the days gone by, you may want to add a little strained honey or a bit of sugar.

Lemon balm and bergamot are two which must be gently boiled for about five minutes. It is better to use an enamel or glass kettle when making those which must be boiled. This helps extract the full flavor. Elderberry blossoms also make a more fragrant tea if simmered for a few minutes. Herb teas are green teas, so in brewing you must judge by taste, not color.

Storing Herbs for Tea

Herbs which are to be used alone or for tisanes for adding to commercial teas should be freshly picked and pressed tightly into jars when in full leaf. They should be turned out every day or two for at least a week to prevent mold. When thoroughly dry, the tins or jars should be kept tightly closed.

While the herbs are growing, you might like to make some fresh herb-flavored teas. I do not know how the experts prepare them, but I have developed my own lazy method, and our friends seem satisfied with the results.

Start with one or two ounces of the best tea that you can afford. A variety not too strongly flavored in itself is best. We like gunpowder, or a good plain green or black tea. Put the tea in a quarter-pound canister, and fill with fresh leaves or blossoms of the herb or flower you have chosen. You may like blossoms of elderberry, a fragrant variety of rose,

123

jasmine or orange blossom. In fact, you may wish a jar of each. As to leaves, peppermint, spearmint, lemon mint or lemon balm, lemon verbena, rose geranium—all are good. Cover the canister. Now, remember to turn out the contents of each once or twice a day, stir well and return to the container. When the leaves or petals are thoroughly dried, your work is over. The joy of partaking begins. Since this method gives highly concentrated flavors, you may want either to mix each packet with a larger amount of tea, or label your boxes and add a small amount of any of them to a pot of tea as you brew it. Because space is limited, the latter is the method I prefer. It is nice to add a dried flower to each cup of flower-flavored tea.

Our tea cupboard amuses those who come to call. It consists of three small shelves originally designed for cookbooks. Now that my collection of cookbooks has reached three well-rounded figures, the shelves have been given over to teas and individual tea pots. Each guest chooses his own.

Cooling Cups of Herbs

Sprigs of orange mint or lemon balm, spearmint or borage may be added to almost any iced drink. A spray of borage flowers is especially pretty in a glass of lemonade. But here is another idea—an herb punch. You will find it delicious!

Herb Punch

1 large handful lemon balm
2 large handfuls borage
Syrup made of 1 cup sugar
    boiled with ½ cup water
3 quarts ginger ale
1 large handful mint

1 quart strong tea
Juice of 6 lemons and 2
    oranges
1 cup pineapple or any other
    fruit juice

Pour 1½ quarts boiling water over lemon balm. Let steep 20 minutes. Strain onto borage and mint; add fruit juices, tea and syrup. Let stand overnight or at least 8 hours. Strain. Add a large piece of ice, and at the last minute, a fresh bunch of mint and the ginger ale.

A friend from India gave me this recipe for an unusual cooling drink:

Sharbatee Gulab

5 large fragrant roses in full
    bloom
2 quarts cold water
1⅓ cups sugar
Finely crushed ice

¼ cup lemon juice
3 cups crushed pineapple (fresh
    or canned)
Rose petals

Wash roses and shake excess water from them. Pluck off petals and place them in a large bowl. Pour cold water over them, cover and let stand in dark cool place (not refrigerator) for 4 hours. Strain. To water add sugar which has been dissolved in lemon juice. Stir, add pineapple. Pour over crushed ice. Place a fresh rose petal on top of each glass. Serves 6 to 8.

Making herb tea

Flower petals

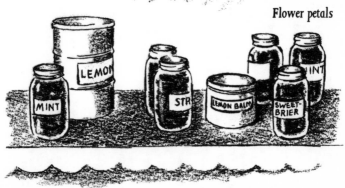

NAME	TYPE	HEIGHT	START FROM:	USES	CULTIVATING HINTS
Angelica	B	6'	Seed or plants	Fresh leaves: with fish. Stalk: as vegetable or sweetened and stewed like rhubarb. Roots: flavor drinks.	Plant seed very early or buy plants.
Anise	A,I	2'	Seed	Fresh leaves: soup, sauce, salad. Dried seeds: breads, cookies.	Plant seed early and thin out when well started.
Basil (a) sweet (b) bush (c) curly	A,I	1-2'	Seed	Curly basil: vinegar, potpourris, tomato dishes. Cooked with everything but sweets.	Pinch out tips of bush basil for bushy growth. Will live over the winter in the house and will set seed when set outdoors.
Bay	P,I	Small tree	Seed or plants	Leaves: in meat, stew, salads, poultry and many vegetables.	May be wintered in house if planted in a tub.
Bergamot	P	2-3'	Seed, root division	In teas and other drinks.	Sow in November; likes shade and moist soil.
Borage	A,I	2'	Seed	Young fresh leaves in iced drinks, salad, tea, many vegetables. Flowers may be candied.	Comes up every year as it self-sows. Very pretty blue flowers.
Burnet	P,I	2'	Seed, root division	Fresh leaves: salads, beverages, vinegar. Dried leaves: tea.	Does not transplant well; seed very early.
Camomile	A	1'	Seed	Flowers: herb teas (German variety), shampoo.	Self-sows; plant in fall or very early spring.
Caraway	B	2'	Seed	Leaves: cheese, salad, soup, meat. Seeds: cookies, cheese, cake, beverages.	Plant in fall for early seed crop the next year; self-sows.
Catnip	P	2'	Seed, root division	Leaves in herb teas. Cats love to roll in it.	Semi-shade; self-sows and spreads by roots.
Chervil	A	1¼'	Seed	Leaves: seasoning and garnish.	Keep out of the very hot sun. Replant each year.
Chives	P,I	1¼'	Bulblets or plants	Use in salad or anything that is improved by a mild onion flavor.	Don't bother with seed. Buy a pot at the grocery. Beautiful purple pompons.

Note: A—annual, B—biennial, P—perennial, I—may be grown indoors.

NAME	TYPE	HEIGHT	START FROM:	USES	CULTIVATING HINTS
Cicely, sweet	P	2-3'	Seed, root division	Salads.	Plant seeds in early fall, or divide last year's roots in the spring.
Coriander	A	1'	Seed	Seed: meat, cheese, soup, salad, cookies.	Seed falls as it ripens, so it must be harvested carefully.
Costmary	P	3'	Seed, root division	Leaves: cakes, meat and tea.	Grows from the roots like rhubarb.
Cress (Garden) (Upland)	A	½'	Seed Seed	Peppery in salad. Good for the canary. Salads.	Keep cut to assure new growth. Treat upland cress as an annual unless you are growing it to produce seed.
Dill	A	3'	Seed	Seeds and leaves: dill pickles, sauerkraut, salad, sauces.	Self-seeds and grows abundantly. Europeans use the foliage for seasoning as well as the seeds.
Dittany	P	2½'	Seed, cutting	Fragrant odor of lemon and spice.	
Fennel (sweet) (wild)	P P	2' 4-6'	Seed Seed	Leaves: fish. Stalks: eaten raw. Seeds: in fish, eggs, cheese, cakes, vegetables. Use to season.	Tall, heavy foliage makes a nice back-ground plant.
Garlic	P	2'	Bulblets (cloves)	Favorite flavoring for many foods. To be rubbed in the salad bowl.	Once established, plants will last for yeers.
Germander	P	1-2'	Seed, root division, cuttings	A lovely hedge.	Replant every few years.
Horehound	P	1½'	Seed	Leaves and flowers in candy, cake, sauces, meat stew, tea.	Plant each year if it winter-kills.
Hyssop	P	2'	Seed, root division, cuttings	Leaves, stems and flowers in medicinal teas, and in vegetables and stews.	Keep trimmed for better growth of leaves.
Lavender	P,I	1'	Seed, plants, root division	Sachets, potpourris, perfume.	Bring inside in winter in cold climates.

Note: A—annual, B—biennial, P—perennial, I—may be grown indoors.

NAME	TYPE	HEIGHT	START FROM:	USES	CULTIVATING HINTS
Lemon balm	P,I	1-2'	Seed, roots	Leaves: tea, iced drinks, potpourris, sachets. In floral bouquets.	Self-sows and spreads by roots.
Lemon verbena	P,I	6'	Buy plant	Grown for fragrance. Little culinary value.	May be kept small in tub if well trimmed.
Lovage	P	5-7'	Seed, root division	Leaves: flavoring meat and vegetable dishes. Stalks: eat raw like celery. It has celery flavor. Seed: cakes, bread, candy.	Start seed indoors in September, set plants out in spring.
Marigold, pot	A,I	1-2'	Seed	Seasoning sea food chowders, meats, puddings. Use the flowers themselves.	Seed early.
Marjoram (sweet)	P,I	½-1'	Seed, roots	A favorite seasoning for all meats and sauces. Use in anything except sweets.	Slow to start; use indoor flat; often winter-kills.
Mint (a) Peppermint (b) Spearmint (c) Applemint	P,I	1-2'	Roots, plant cuttings	Used for flavoring. Leaves used in beverages. Mint juleps are made with spearmint. Teas. Sauce for lamb.	Keep different kinds of mint apart as they tend to cross and change their flavor. A metal edging sunk a few inches around the bed will keep them from overrunning the yard.
Nasturtium	A	1'	Seed	Flowers as a garnish; stems and leaves in tart salads; seeds as a condiment. Seasoning teas.	Keep flowers picked for more blooms. Double hybrids do not set seed.
Oregano (wild marjoram)	P	1'	Seed, roots	Actually wild marjoram. A favorite in Italy for seasoning many things.	Grows wild in Mexico. Only an inferior oregano grows in the United States.
Parsley	B,I	1'	Seed	Put in anything but sweets. A pretty garnish. Use in bouquets.	Will set seed the second year if allowed to grow undisturbed through the winter.
Pennyroyal	P	1½'	Root cuttings, root division	A pungent tea, but not generally used for seasoning because of strong flavor.	Spreads rapidly, a good ground cover. Unlike other mints, grows prostrate.
Rose geranium	P,I	1-3'	Stem cuttings or plants	Use leaves to flavor jellies, in desserts, in tea, sachets and potpourris.	Keep a new supply of plants growing from cuttings.
Rosemary	P,I	3-5'	Seed, plants, stem cuttings	Fresh and dried leaves are a gourmet seasoning in roasts, fried potatoes, jelly. Pungent pine-like odor.	Start root cuttings in wet sand. Take indoors in the winter. Likes sun and gravelly soil.

Note: A—annual, B—biennial, P—perennial, I—may be grown indoors.

NAME	TYPE	HEIGHT	START FROM:	USES	CULTIVATING HINTS
Rue	P	2'	Seed, cuttings, root division	The musty-flavored leaves are not popular in the United States. Pretty border or low hedge.	Hardy.
Sage	P	2'	Seed, by cuttings or root division	Flavoring for poultry dressing, cheese, tea.	Cut back for new growth.
Santolina	P	2'	Plants, layering	Formerly used as a moth repellent, but today mostly popular as an edging.	
Savory (a) Summer (b) Winter	A,I A,I	1½' 1¼'	Root division	Dried leaves: meats, soup, stew, omelette, beans, tomatoes. Less delicate flavor than summer savory, but used on fish and green beans.	Killed by first freeze; does well in poor soil. Woodier than summer savory; nice to take inside.
Shallots	A,I	1½'	Bulblets	Use for flavoring as you would onions.	Flower stem stays erect after the leaves fall.
Sorrel (garden)	P	2-3'	Seed	Use the leaves as salad or greens.	Easy to start from seed.
Tansy	P	2-4'	Seed	Flavors pudding or tea.	Plant seed in autumn for early crop. Makes a mass of foliage.
Tarragon	P,I	1½'	Plants or root division	Vinegar, salads, fish, poultry.	Seed does not set on true tarragon in America. Protect in winter.
Thyme	P,I	½-1'	Seed, cuttings, root division, layering	*T. vulgaris* is the best for flavoring out of the 60 varieties known. Potpourris. Use in anything but sweets.	Mulch over the winter. For an early spring growth start seeds indoors.
Woodruff, sweet	P	1'	Seed, root division	Sachets, flavors for beverages.	A ground cover in shady woodland. Start root cuttings in wet sand.

Note: A—annual, B—biennial, P—perennial, I—may be grown indoors.

131

Part III.
GARDEN CRAFTING

Bird basin on tree stump

Flowers or herbs

11.

PERSONAL TOUCHES IN YOUR GARDEN

When you want a room to look lived in and loved, you put pictures on the walls, gay pillows on the sofa, books and plants and flowers on the tables. You are pleased when friends say that your home reflects your personality. They will say the same thing about your garden if you add interesting touches which make it truly yours.

BRING BIRDS TO YOUR GARDEN

Spread out a welcome mat for the birds and they will be a constant joy to you. They will repay you with song, and will help keep harmful insects away from the plants in your garden.

Offer the birds rent-free houses, as simple or as fancy as you please, and you will have delightful tenants. Put up your

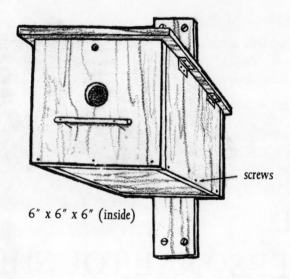

6" x 6" x 6" (inside)

screws

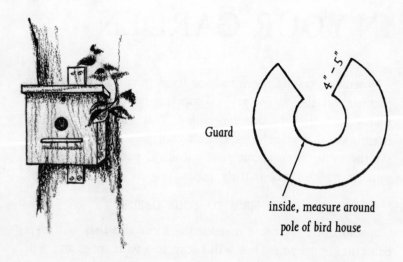

Bird house

Guard

4" – 5"

inside, measure around
pole of bird house

birdhouses in the fall, so that by the time the birds return in the spring, the houses will be weathered enough to blend into the landscape. Birds are sometimes timid about entering too-new houses.

It isn't difficult to make a birdhouse if you can do a bit of carpentering. Use boards that are heavy enough so that they will not warp out of shape after repeatedly being soaked by rain and then dried out by the sun. Wood is the best material to use because it will keep the nest warm on cool nights, and fairly cool when the sun is hot. A metal birdhouse, for instance, would become an oven in the hot sun, but you can use narrow tin strips to seal the cracks between wooden boards and keep out the rain.

For ventilation, drill a couple of small holes in protected spots under the eaves. It's also a good idea to hinge the roof of the birdhouse, so that you can lift it up and clean house after the birds have flown south in the fall.

If you are making a wren house, trace around a coin 1 inch in diameter to get the correct size for the opening. A 2-inch hole will suit martins, and a $1\frac{1}{2}$-inch coin makes just the right size doorway for a bluebird.

Martins are very sociable birds. They live in colonies, and so they like multiple dwellings, but each little "apartment" must have its own private entrance. However, do not place houses for wrens and bluebirds in close proximity to each other. Each pair wants space of its own, and they will fight off other birds who try to trespass.

It is easy and enjoyable to design a birdhouse, if you are going to make one yourself. You can make one quite simply of rectangular pieces or squares of board. Or, if you have grown some large gourds in your garden, let them dry out thoroughly and you can turn them into admirable birdhouses. Just cut a doorway large enough for the birds to enter, and a tiny hole or two for ventilation.

Place the birdhouse where cats and squirrels can't reach it. Be careful not to put it under a wire or clothesline, or an overhanging branch, for squirrels can walk across even a single wire and then drop or jump onto the birdhouse.

BIRD FEEDERS

Both you and the birds will get a lot of pleasure from a bird feeder. Place it where you can watch it through the window. Mount it on a post that is tall enough so that cats cannot jump up onto it, but not too high to reach when you put out a fresh supply of food.

Attach a baffle to the post a foot or more·below the feed board. This is a conical piece of tin, sloping downward, to prevent climbing animals from reaching the feed board.

The feed board itself can be quite simple. Make it about 12 to 15 inches square, with a protected bin for food on the north side of the board. (This will leave the sunny south end for the birds to sit on while they are eating.) Use a heavy wire mesh screening, leaving a ½-inch space at the bottom,

Pie tin

Lid

Pie tin

9"

6"

Cake pan

Tree branch

Molded
concrete
bath

to hold the food in the bin. Frame the edge of the feed board
with a ½-inch rim of tin or wood slats to prevent the birds
from scratching the feed off onto the ground.

If you really want to see the birds feeding at close range,
mount the feeder right on the outer sill of a sunny window.
The kitchen window is best. Suspend wires to support the
outer edge of the board, or brace it from below with wood
or metal braces. You won't need a food reservoir, since you
can open the window and place food on the board whenever
it is needed.

Birds will patronize your window feeder most willingly
if there is a tree or a tall bush nearby. Then they will be able to
alight in the tree and look the situation over before descending
to feed.

BIRD BATHS

A bird bath not only attracts birds to drink and splash about
in the water, but also makes an attractive addition to the
garden. If your yard happens to have a tree stump in it, it
will make a good base. Otherwise you will have to sink a

post, but be sure it is large enough and set in firmly enough to support the bath basin without danger of its tipping over.

The easiest way to make a permanent bird bath is with ready-mix cement. All you have to do is add water, according to the directions on the bag, and pour the mixture into the lid of a garbage can. As soon as the cement begins to harden and hold its shape, scoop it hollow to form the basin. The basin should taper from a depth of ½ inch near the rim to 2 inches in the middle. Leave the bottom fairly rough, so that the birds can get a good foothold. If you wish, you can decorate the bath by pushing little pebbles into the cement before it sets. When the cement is completely dry, the bath will come out of the can lid quite easily.

If your yard is so well protected that there is no danger that stray cats will disturb the birds, you can place a bird bath directly on the ground. Even an old pie tin will entice the birds on a hot, sunny day, but it will be best to paint the inside with a dark flat paint to dull the surface. If you sprinkle in some sand while the paint is still wet, the birds will get a better footing.

Plant some mint around the bird bath, and perhaps some petunias which will flower almost all summer. Splash out the water each day and replace it with fresh water, and scrub out the bird bath with a stiff brush every once in a while.

A GARDEN POOL

Let a small pool be the focal point of your garden. All you need is a wood or tin wash tub. If you don't have one in the cellar or attic, try the nearest Salvation Army store or an antique store or junk yard.

Choose a suitable spot and dig a hole deep enough to hold the tub with only three inches extending above ground level.

If you paint the tub first, it will help protect it from the weather, and a blue or green pool will blend naturally into your garden.

Around the pool you can plant flowers in a careless, informal fashion, or you can use the pool as the central feature of a rock garden. Or, if you have been wondering where to keep your house plants during the summer, you can surround the pool with potted plants.

A water lily will look lovely in the pool. You can get one in a pot, all ready to put down in the tub, or you can buy a plastic lily or two which will look quite natural floating on the water and blend nicely with any real flowers growing around the edge. You can perch a ceramic animal or bird on the edge of the pool, just for fun.

If you have an umbrella plant in your indoor garden, it will enjoy a summer vacation in the pool. Hang its pot over the edge of the pool. You can make a support for it out of a wire coat hanger or a piece of heavy-gauge wire. Twist the wire around the pot and hook it over the edge of the pool

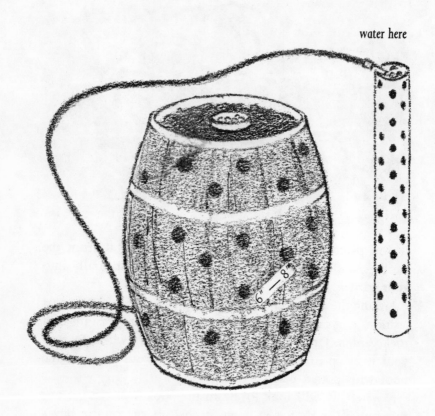

water here

8"

6"

Strawberry barrel

so that the water comes up over the top. Let the pot lean against the side of the pool for support.

A STRAWBERRY BARREL

A strawberry bed takes up a lot of space in a garden, but if you really love strawberries, why not make a strawberry barrel? It will only occupy a few square feet.

Get the largest barrel you can find. Drill drainage holes in the bottom of the barrel and leave the other end open. Now drill holes, from 2 to 4 inches in diameter, in the sides of the barrel. They should be about 6 to 8 inches apart, and the bottom row of holes should be about 9 inches from the ground.

Inside the barrel stand an old stovepipe or drainpipe which has been punched full of holes. Fill the pipe with small rocks. It will now stand erect while you fill the barrel. First put 3 inches of gravel in the bottom of the barrel, and then fill the barrel all the way up with rich soil.

Your barrel is now ready to be planted. Simply insert a strawberry plant in each hole. To water the plants, run water into the drain pipe with a hose, or pour it in with a bucket.

A WROUGHT-IRON GARDEN BENCH

It's nice to have a place to sit and admire your garden. It is especially nice to sit on a handsome and unusual bench which you have made yourself. Here is an idea for a bench which will be the envy of your friends.

While you are in the second-hand store or junk yard looking for a wash tub for your pool, see whether you can find an old treadle sewing machine. You don't need the machine itself, but most of them have very attractive iron sides, and these two pieces of patterned iron-work are just what you need. Simply "plant" them in your garden, about 18 inches apart, put a heavy board across them, and there is your bench. You can paint the bench white or green or red—whatever looks best in your garden.

Some of the old sewing machines have iron sides which are too tall for a bench. If you find one like that, you can make a useful garden table instead. You can make a small table by using short boards, or a nice long picnic table if you use long boards.

Wrought-iron garden table

Trellises for vine or flower screens

TRELLISES FOR CLIMBERS

There are often problem areas in a garden which you wish to screen from view. Take an ugly garage wall, for instance, or perhaps a compost heap. You can't remove the offender, but you can hide it with vines.

For a hurry-up cover-up of a garage or wall, start with morning glory seeds and hollyhocks. Plant the hollyhocks in front of, and alternating with, the morning glories. While you are waiting for them to come up, run a string or a light wire from stakes in the ground to nails at the top of the garage in lace-the-corset fashion. It won't be long before you have a lovely covering of vines and flowers. Pink and white hollyhocks would look beautiful against Heavenly Blue morning glories.

A more substantial trellis is needed if you wish to screen off a vacant lot or an ugly building where there is not enough room for shrubbery. As the vines grow, tie them to the trellis if they seem to need support. For lightweight vines you can use soft twine, raffia, plastic ties, wire ties enclosed in paper, or old nylon hose cut in strips. For heavy-stemmed vines, use insulated wire, clothesline, strips of canvas or lengths of old nylon hose.

To choose which vines to plant, look through seed catalogs and consult the clerks at the seed store or nursery. You have to consider the climate, whether the vines will be in a sunny or shaded location, what kinds of leaves and flowers you want, etc. There are hundreds of varieties to choose from. Some are unusual, some have beautiful flowers, and still others will make your garden fragrant. Here are a few which you may not know:

Canary vine: The soft yellow flower of this annual vine looks like a bird from some angles.

Moonflowers: The white flowers are big and showy. An annual.

Balloon vine: The seed pods look like little balloons. An annual.

Wisteria: This is such a romantic vine! It will remind you of ladies in hoop skirts, and Southern mansions. Its flowers are pale hyacinth blue, and fragrant. The vine grows larger each year, forming a gnarled trunk.

Scarlet runner bean: This vine has gay red flowers which may be cut and taken into the house for bouquets. If you leave them to form seed pods, you can eat the beans.

Hearts-and-honey: This vine is fun because the flowers change from pinkish orange to rose-pink in a day!

Black-eyed-Susan vine: The blossoms are not related to the wildflowers that grow in the autumn fields. The vine has white, yellow and orange flowers, each with a dark eye in the middle.

Cup-and-saucer vine: When you see its flowers, you will know where this vine got its name.

Canary vine

Cup-and-saucer vine

Garden paths can do a lot to enhance the appearance of your garden, especially if you choose the right materials. A brick wall, for example, goes well in a Victorian or any old-fashioned garden. You can set the bricks in the usual brickwork pattern, or in a checkerboard, or a chevron pattern. Dig a foundation, and then fill in the spaces between the bricks with sand or with well-packed sod.

Stepping stones are particularly suitable across a grassy lawn leading to a pool. You can buy flat rocks or slate from a stone quarry, or you may be able to find suitable rocks in a field or along a country road. (Before taking rocks from a field, be sure to ask permission of the owners.) To start such a path, dig slight depressions in which to lay each stone. Measure the distance from one stone to the next by walking and placing a marker at each step.

You can make a garden path of gravel and edge it with low-growing flowers and herbs. Use aluminum stripping to confine the gravel.

In planning your paths, remember that they need not be straight unless you want them that way as part of a design. Curving paths are often more interesting, and they tend to give a casual air to your garden.

Gravel garden path

Flat stones

PEBBLES AND STONES

Farmers dig rocks out of their fields and vegetable gardeners sift the pebbles out of their seedbeds. But there is a place for both rocks and pebbles in a flower garden.

A big boulder looks charming surrounded by an irregularly shaped bed of perennial flowers. If your garden does have such a boulder, build the garden around it, and let some of the flowers snuggle up to the rock. Otherwise, the family can make quite a project out of getting a big boulder and placing it in a good spot.

Use pebbles and small stones to edge a small garden pool. Larger rocks, just big enough to handle, make a fine edging for a garden path. You can whitewash them or leave them natural.

Keep your eyes open for attractive and unusual stones, and collect them for use in your garden. You may even get interested in rock collecting as an extra hobby!

Here is an idea that uses stones to solve the problem of a difficult corner of the yard or alongside the house where you can't get lawn to grow properly. Arrange fairly flat stones over the area, with spaces in between them. Plant flowers in the spaces and you will have a beautiful spot that might otherwise have been an eyesore.

147

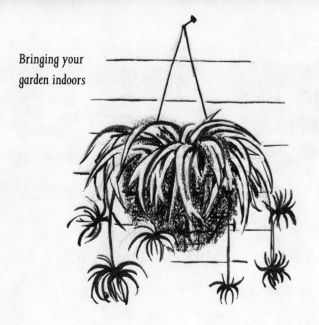

Bringing your
garden indoors

12. WINTER GARDENS

When the cold winds begin to blow, it is time to bring the garden indoors, or at least to refurbish your house plants and perhaps add a few new ones. You probably know most of the usual house plants such as ivy and philodendron, so you will surely welcome an introduction to some of the more unusual varieties. These plants are not rare or expensive, but each one has some unusual feature which makes it fascinating to grow.

SPIDER PLANT

A spider plant does not spin a web; neither does it bite. Put it on a high shelf or in a hanging pot and it will weave a web of enchantment.

The plant has long narrow leaves, white-striped and graceful. It bears small lily-like flowers which grow on runners. The runners trail down as much as 2 feet below the parent plant. Keep your eye on the tips of the runners, for soon new plantlets will appear, looking like spiders.

When the new plantlets measure 2 or 3 inches across, you can remove them and start new plants. Plant them in water or dirt and soon they, too, will have new "spiders" hatching out.

PICKABACK PLANT

The pickaback plant is more interesting than beautiful, although it can be rather attractive if you keep it from getting straggly. The baby plants ride pickaback on the mother plant, forming at the tips of the leaf stalks. When you see this plant, you will know why it is sometimes called "mother-of-thousands."

Since this plant can go without sunlight for quite a long time, you can grow it in a north window, or even away from a window on a table or bookcase.

"Mother-of-thousands"

VENUS'-FLYTRAP

Have you ever seen a plant that catches its own dinner? The Venus'-flytrap does! The ends of its leaves are real traps. They are fringed at the edges, and inside there are a few extremely sensitive hairs which serve as triggers. When an unwary insect brushes against them, the trap closes on its victim. An acid fluid then digests the insect.

It takes about eight days for the plant to digest its meal. Then the trap opens again. You can spring the trap with a pencil or other object, but if you play with it too much you will wear it out.

PRAYER PLANT

This plant has large velvety leaves of pale green splotched with chocolate brown. As the plant grows older, the splotches turn to dark green. The leaves grow at right angles to the stem during the daytime, but they change position at night. Watch them carefully when it gets dark and you will see them move slowly upright. All night long they reach up, like arms stretched in prayer. In the morning they return to their daytime position.

The prayer plant is easy to grow. It likes rich soil and plenty of moisture, especially on its leaves. Spray them each day. Keep the plant in partial shade, with sun only part of the morning or afternoon.

AN AIR PLANT

There are several plants which seem to grow on nothing but air. "Miracle leaf" is one of the most interesting. Bryophyllum is its botanical name.

Take a leaf from this plant and pin it to a curtain, or place it on a window sill. Before long you will have tiny new plants

Prayer plant—its leaves
reach up "in prayer" at night

growing around the edge of the leaf. First you will see little
hairlike roots forming in the notches, then the smallest of
new leaves.

After a new little plant has grown about 1 inch tall, you
can cut it away from the mother leaf, snipping a bit of the old
leaf along with the new plant. Lay it on top of the soil in a
flowerpot with just a sprinkling of soil over the roots. Keep
it moist, and you will soon have a healthy new plant.

Set Bryophyllum outdoors in the spring and let it grow
large and straggly. New plants do not grow on leaves which
are still attached to the old plant. When the weather begins to
turn cold, pick a dozen or so of the leaves to give away as
gifts. Even though this plant is not very beautiful, it is so
fascinating that each friend who sees it will want a leaf to
grow. You can even send the leaves through the mail.

FUNNY NAME PLANTS

Here are some plants that are easy to grow which may appeal to you because of their amusing names:

The *seersucker plant* has fleshy, quilted leaves of dark metallic green with bands of pale gray. The underside of the leaf is red.

The *snake plant* has tall spiky leaves of dark green with creamy green bands. It is practically indestructible, and thrives on neglect. The roots send up new plants a few inches away, which you can transplant.

Snake plant

Two-men-in-a-boat has long, narrow leaves of dark green with purple undersides growing from a single thick stem. Flowers grow at the base of the leaves in boat-shaped bracts, and there are two little men in each boat! This plant is also known as Moses, or Moses-on-a-raft.

PALMS

How would you like to have a palm tree growing in your living room? Of course, you don't want a tall palm, such as you see in semi-tropical lands, but a nice little palm tree.

Palm tree

As a house plant, it will stay within the bounds of a pot for years. The fronds are pretty, and if you are very lucky, some day your palm may flower.

SUCCULENTS

Succulents are among the easiest of all house plants to grow. In fact, the hardest part is choosing among the many delightful varieties. You will surely want to grow a few.

Jade plant: When you buy a jade plant it will probably come in a 2-inch flowerpot, but it will grow and grow over the years. In about ten years or so it will be big enough for a large pot, or a small tub. Then you may have a delightful surprise, early some spring, if the plant decides to put out its fragrant pink and white blossoms.

The plant needs good drainage, plenty of fresh air and not too much water. When the plant is small you may need to water it every other day, but as it grows larger, the thick leaves hold moisture and the plant needs water only once or twice a week.

If the leaves drop, let the plant dry out, and then give it more fresh air and pinch back shoots which have gotten too

Jade plant

long and straggly. In the fall—perhaps from September to December—the plant will rest. You should water it less often and keep it in a cooler place. You will know when the jade plant starts to rest because it will stop putting out fresh growth.

Crown of thorns: This is the happiest plant you ever saw. It blooms and blooms, month after month. The gay red flowers grow in clusters among inch-long thorns and tiny bright green leaves. It likes sandy soil, full sunlight, and not too much water. The spiny stems grow almost vinelike after a while, and you may want to train them around a hoop or trellis. Bend a wire coat hanger into any shape you want, then straighten out the hook and poke it into the soil. When the plant asks for a rest by dropping its leaves, give it less water still until it begins to grow again.

Panda plant: The blue-green leaves of this easy-to-grow succulent have a thick coat of furry white hairs, tipped at the edges with chocolate brown. It will really remind you of the panda at the zoo.

Coral beads: Row upon row of bright red beads grow on upright stalks. The color is brightest if you keep the plant in the sun. You can start new plants from old beads.

CACTUS PLANTS

Cactus plants have many unusual forms, and many shades of green to give them interest, but they are especially fascinating on the rather rare occasions when they put forth exotic, tropical blooms. They thrive in dry or sandy soil, and they make ideal house plants for even the most absent-minded gardener, because they do not mind being neglected. Give them plenty of sun, but little water and very little earth to grow in.

Arrange an assortment of cacti in a shallow container, or grow individual plants in small pots with plenty of broken brick underneath sandy soil. Water once, thoroughly, to settle the soil, and then water only once or twice a week.

African violets

FLOWERING PLANTS

If you want to be sure of flowers on your house plants, you will have to stick to the tried-and-true kinds which most people grow in their homes. Any of the following will fill your home with brightness and cheer during the "indoor" months:

African violets	gloxinia
amaryllis	impatiens
begonia	Jerusalem cherry
geranium	lantana
wax plant	bulbs—hyacinth, daffodil, crocus, narcissus

Hyacinth

Amaryllis

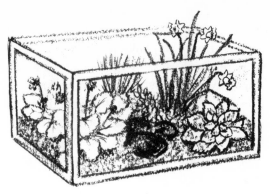

Terrarium—a miniature garden enclosed in glass

TERRARIUM

A terrarium is a miniature garden enclosed in glass. You can use a fish tank or bowl, a large goblet or any glass or plastic container which will let light through. If you give your artistic tendencies full sway when you design and plant your terrarium, you can achieve a lovely miniature landscape.

Although a terrarium is easy to set up, it is not always simple to keep the plants alive. Do not be disappointed if your first effort does not survive all winter. Profit by your mistakes and start a new one.

Begin with a 1-inch layer of gravel, charcoal or similar material in the bottom of the container to provide drainage. If your yard or nearby woods has soft green moss growing, dig some up to line the sides of the bowl, moss side out, to the height of the soil. This is not really necessary, but it looks nice.

Next comes the soil. Mix equal parts of garden soil, sand and peat moss and pour it into the bowl unevenly. Let it slope from back to front, or press it into two or three little hills.

Now add plants, rocks, pottery figures, twigs or pieces of

bark to the scene, according to your plans. You may need a pair of tweezers to set the plants in place if the bowl is deep, or narrow at the neck. If you get soil on the leaves, brush them off carefully. Spray the whole arrangement lightly with a little sprinkler, and then cover the container with a sheet of glass or plastic film. You will not have to water it often for the soil to remain moist. If the bowl becomes foggy, open the cover slightly until the extra water evaporates. Keep the terrarium in bright light but not in the sun.

What can you grow in a terrarium? These plants grow well:

African violets	ferns
begonia	ivy
coleus	peperomia
corn plant (cracaenas)	violets
crotons	wandering Jew
evergreen seedlings	partridgeberry
lichen	trillium

You might try planting some fern spores in your terrarium. You will find them in tiny pockets on the underside of fern fronds. Find a fern with fat, ripe spores and shake a few into your terrarium. They will start as a flat green growth and then ferns will sprout.

WATER GARDEN

A water garden is very decorative, and easy as can be to grow. You need a broad, flat container such as a molded plastic tray, although a flat soup plate will do for a smaller garden. Paint the inside blue, if possible, and when the paint is dry add water and plenty of rocks. Some of the rocks should be big enough to protrude several inches above the water. Group them together attractively, leaving clear lakes and ponds here and there.

Water garden

Place your plants among the rocks, pushing the rocks into place to support them. Cuttings of ivy, philodendron, pachysandra and wandering Jew will all root themselves and grow well in water, and so will many bulbs. Add a few jonquils, narcissi or autumn croci to make your garden gay.

DESERT GARDEN

You can use any kind of container, from a cup to a tray, for a desert garden. Mix equal parts of sand and soil and arrange a collection of miniature cactus plants over your desert. Model a little adobe hut out of clay, and try to find a tiny ceramic burro to live nearby in the garden.

Desert garden

If you plan to move your house plants outdoors for the summer, choose a warm sunny day in spring and give them their first airing in the sun for a few hours. Gradually leave them out for longer periods, while they are getting used to differences in temperatures. When all danger of frost is past, you can leave them out day and night.

If you use your plants to decorate porch, patio or terrace you need not change their containers. However, if you wish to plant them in the garden, you should remove plants from fancy containers and put them into ordinary clay pots. (Do not plant them directly into the soil, or the roots will grow out of bounds.) Sink the clay pots into holes deep enough to allow just a bit of rim above ground. If the weather is quite dry, or if you plan to go away during the summer, it is a good idea to cover the top of the soil with peat moss to retain as much moisture as possible.

In the fall, when it is time to take your house plants back in, you may find that some of them have outgrown their old containers. Replant those that seem root-bound in slightly larger containers.

Moving indoor plants
outdoors for summer

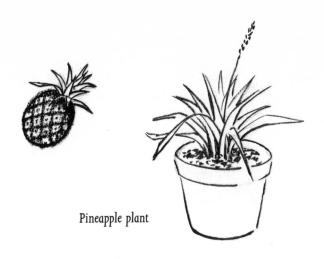

Pineapple plant

13. GARDENS FROM LEFTOVERS

The vegetable kingdom holds many surprises in store for those who love to experiment and try new things. If you know what to look for, your kitchen will yield unsuspected possibilities for unusual house plants. Did you know that you can grow beautiful plants from the parts of vegetables and fruits that are usually thrown away? It's fun to watch them grow, and they make intriguing conversation pieces.

PINEAPPLE

A fresh pineapple is a lot of trouble to prepare, but it makes delicious eating, and the pleasure will last still longer if you save the spiny top section. You won't be able to raise pineapples, but you can grow a pineapple plant.

Remove a row or two of the lower leaves and let the cut end dry for a couple of days. Then plant it about 1 inch deep in a flowerpot. It will grow very slowly, so you will not have to worry about its getting too large for a long, long time. Find a sunny haven for it, water it frequently, and do not be discouraged if nothing happens for as long as a month or two. Eventually it will grow into a deep green rosette with saw-toothed, spiky leaves. In the summer you can set it outdoors in a sunny spot, and then bring it indoors before the frost sets in.

A pineapple top makes an attractive table decoration, especially if you surround it with other plants to form a dish garden. It will be particularly attractive if it blooms, and it just might if you fertilize it well, but always water it before feeding it. If blossoms do appear, they will look like miniature pineapples with blue and red spots.

AVOCADO

A fine, green avocado plant is a joy to behold, and you can grow one from a pit. The growth is slow, however, and you will need lots of patience. Do not give up if you see no signs of life for many weeks!

Choose a nice fat seed from a ripe avocado. If you find one that is beginning to split, you are in luck. One end of the seed will be a little larger than the other, and slightly flattened. That end goes down. Set it into a jar whose neck is small enough to hold the pit so that you can keep the bottom end under water. Otherwise, you can poke toothpicks into the seed to keep it from falling into the jar.

Important! Keep the jar filled to the very brim. Never let the bottom of the seed get dry. And when the roots sprout, never, never let them dry out, or the plant will die. Until

Avocado plant

the roots are well formed, it is a good idea to keep the jar near the kitchen sink so that you will remember to add water each morning, and again in the evening if necessary.

It will take three or four weeks, or even longer, before the base of the seed splits open and strong white roots appear. The roots will grow fairly rapidly, and may fill up the jar before the top of the seed breaks open and the green leaves begin to grow.

Once your little tree is growing well and has several leaves on it, you can transfer it to a pot of soil. Plant it shallowly, with about one-third of the pit above the soil. Water your plant every day without fail, or the leaves will droop pathetically. If you do discover that you have forgotten to water it, set the pot in a pan of water so that the water can soak up from the bottom.

Some avocado pits just won't sprout, no matter how kind you are to them, so it is a good idea to start several at the same time. You can give away the extras as gifts.

During the summer months you can plunge the entire pot into the ground in the garden, but be sure to bring it indoors in the fall. The avocado is a tender plant, but it will reward you by growing tall and beautiful, with large, shapely leaves.

DATE PALMS

Are you good at remembering dates? To grow date palms, it's a good idea to forget the date, for they take a while to get started. Just soak six or eight date pits in water for a few days, and then plant them shallowly in a pot of soil or, better yet, in a planter with other plants growing.

And now you can forget about dates. Months later, when you think your dates have "stood you up," you will suddenly discover a tiny date palm coming up.

Date palm

CITRUS FRUITS

Collect half a dozen or so of the plumpest grapefruit seeds you can find and plant them ½ inch deep in a pot of soil. Put the pot in a warm but shaded spot and keep the soil moist until the sprouts appear. Within a few weeks you should see some pushing up through the soil. Then you can move the pot to a bright window.

After the leaves have formed you can transplant them into fancy pots or dishes. Grapefruits are not fussy. They will

Grapefruit

grow in any type of container—clay or plastic, china or metal, wood or ceramic, it's all one to a grapefruit. However, the size of the pot will influence the growth. If you put a sturdy seedling into a large pot, it will grow to a height of 18 or 24 inches. If you put one into a small bowl, you will have an interesting dwarf tree.

You can plant orange and lemon seeds too, but they do not grow so easily, and they take more time to sprout. The little lemon trees are sensitive to temperature changes and drafts.

FRUIT TREES

Many fruit seeds will sprout and grow into trees indoors, but you can never tell what will grow until you try it. Experiment with plum and cherry pits, apple and pear pips, peach stones, prunes, even olives! Put several of one kind in a pot and label it, and then keep your fingers crossed. You might even try nuts in the shell, if they haven't been roasted.

Try planting some fruit pits, seeds or stones.

Save grape seeds for planting!

GRAPES

Grape seeds may be a nuisance when you are eating grapes, but they can be a pleasure later on. Soak a handful of grape seeds for about a week, then plant them in sand or soil. It may take several weeks before the first sprouts appear. When they are well above ground, lift them out carefully with a teaspoon and transplant them to a pretty dish. You will need several seedlings in one dish to get a nice plant, since grape seeds grow into a vine, not a bush.

CARROT

The carrot is a sunny vegetable in more ways than its color. Its top will grow into a pretty plant, and its root will perform tricks too.

Select the biggest carrot you can find—one at least an inch in diameter. Trim off the leaves and stems and cut off the stem end about an inch down from the top of the carrot. Plant the top in sand, soil or water, and it will soon sprout into a feathery plant.

Now for the root end. Hollow it out with a vegetable corer or a sharp, thin-bladed knife such as a pocketknife. You now have an elongated yellow basket, lacking only a handle. Poke holes near the top and attach a handle of raffia

Grow carrot tops

Make baskets out of the roots, and watch them grow!

or string. Now hang the carrot basket in a sunny window and fill it with water. Add water once or twice a day to keep the carrot filled, and watch what happens.

In a week or so the bottom of the basket will begin to sprout. Instead of trailing down, however, the lacy green fronds will turn up and surround the carrot with living basketry!

BEETS

You can grow beet tops in water or soil. Their dark red and green foliage is especially attractive. Try growing a dish of beet tops and carrot tops. They will look lovely together.

You can grow other root vegetables, such as turnips,

rutabagas and parsnips, in exactly the same way. When you trim off the old leaves, if you find any new young leaves starting, leave them on. Then plant the tops, cut side down, in a dish of water or soil. If you can find a horse-radish, it will grow into a plant with unusual arrow-shaped leaves.

TURNIP GARDEN

Did you ever see a turnip garden? Not a garden full of turnips, but a garden planted in a turnip! Find a big, fat turnip, cut off the top and scoop out the root until the shell is just about 1 inch thick. Fill the turnip with soil and plant some soaked beans in it. Put the turnip into a shallow bowl and surround it with peat moss. Water the peat moss and the little garden inside the turnip every day. Soon the garden will start to grow, inside and out, as the beans sprout and the turnip starts sprouting too.

ONIONS

If you find an onion that has started to sprout, don't cook it. Plant it! Even if it has started to grow rotten in the bin,

Sprouting onion

just remove the spoiled outer layers without damaging the sprouts.

Plant the onion in a glass jar or bowl, or even in the earth out of doors in the summertime. The onion shoots will begin growing quickly, and they will twist into weird shapes that will remind you of modern art sculptures.

SWEET-POTATO VINE

Once we planted a sweet potato in a heavy glass bowl. It stood on the piano under a group of four windows, and that vine grew and grew like Jack's beanstalk! First it grew up one window, and then in no time at all it crept across the tops

Sweet potato

of all four windows. We had to help it twine around the end of the curtain pole, and then it cascaded down again, framing the entire group of windows with greenery.

If you want to grow a sweet-potato vine, you have to choose the right kind of sweet potato. Those from the market which have been treated to prevent sprouting are no good, of course, and you cannot use a young, freshly dug sweet potato, either. But if you get an older tuber, it will soon grow.

Place it root end down in a jar of water. The neck of the jar should be small enough so that only the lower half of the sweet potato is inside the jar. Make sure that at least the tip of the sweet potato is always under water. At first it is fun to watch the roots grow, but later on, when the jar is almost solidly filled with roots, you can transfer the potato to a pottery bowl, if you desire.

To start the plant growing, keep it in a cool, dark place for 10 days or until the roots are visible. Then, as the spikes of leaves start forming, pinch some off so that only a few remain. Put the plant on a window sill and stretch strings for the vines to cling to. Because the sweet potato doesn't waste any time about starting to grow, it will give you something to watch while you wait for some of your slower plants to sprout.

GREEN PEPPER PLANTS

All recipes containing green peppers start with the direction, "Discard all seeds." But don't throw them away! Plant some and watch them grow. Simply spread them over the earth, and don't worry if they cling to each other in places, for you can thin them out later. Cover the seeds with a thin layer of soil and water them daily. When the sprouts are about 3 inches high, transplant some to pots. Dig them up carefully with a spoon and move them to their new homes. Even one green pepper will give you seeds for enough plants for yourself and for giving away to friends.

Green pepper

PETER PIPER'S PEPPERS

I don't suppose Peter Piper really picked a peck of pickled peppers, but you can grow lovely house plants by using the pepper seeds from pickling spices. Take a tiny red pepper from a box of mixed pickling spices. Open it and plant the seeds, being careful not to touch your face or rub your eyes after touching the seeds until you have scrubbed your hands.

A glossy green plant will grow, and soon it will be abloom with little star-shaped white flowers. The flowers will turn into tiny green peppers, scarcely an inch long, and gradually the peppers will turn a bright red. As more buds open into flowers, you will have white flowers, green peppers and red peppers all at the same time!

These attractive pepper plants can grow outdoors in a window box or planter in the summertime, and they certainly make dressy house plants during the winter.

Lentils  Lima beans

LENTILS AND BEANS

Save a few lentils or beans before they go into the soup pot. Plant them and they will say thank you by growing very quickly. Simply scatter them in a saucer and add just enough water to cover them. Keep the saucer in a light window and add water very often so that the beans never get dry. Within a week you will have a miniature forest!

GRASS

"And the green grass grew all around." Yes, even indoors. You can grow a patch of grass on a sponge, or on a corncob which has been eaten or scraped clean of kernels.

Lay the corncob in a shallow dish and half fill the dish with water. If the cob is dried, fill the dish full and allow a few hours for the water to soak up. Now sprinkle grass seed

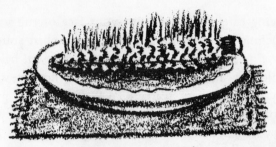

Growing grass on corncobs

generously over the cob. The little pockets which held the
kernels will hold the seed. Add water to the dish daily, and
in about a week's time the grass will begin to grow. You can
let it grow naturally, or trim it smooth or even into shapes.

LETTUCE ON A SPONGE

Place a sponge in a shallow dish of water. Any kind of
sponge will do—rubber, cellulose or plastic. Sprinkle lettuce
seed over the top and pat it down. Put the saucer in a warm
place and keep the sponge wet. Soon you will have pretty
little rosettes of lettuce growing right out of the sponge.

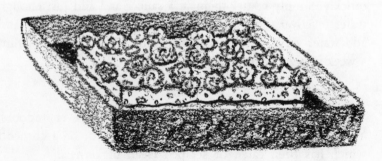

Growing lettuce on a sponge

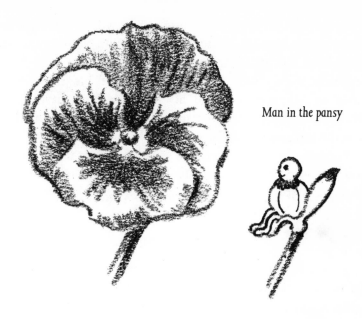

Man in the pansy

14. GARDEN MAGIC

Flowers are delightful to look at, delicious to smell and fun to pick, but there are lots of other ways to have fun with flowers. Here are some novel ideas to try.

LITTLE MAN IN A PANSY

Pansies have faces, but did you know that there is a little man hiding in each flower? Pick a pansy and look for him. Pansies bloom best when they are picked every day, so you will do no harm if you take a few.

Pick a blossom with a long enough stem to hold easily. It does not matter if the bloom is not quite fresh. Very carefully pull off all the colored petals. You will be left with five little green "petals" called the calyx. With your thumbnail snip away the two in front.

There! See the little man? He is sitting in his chair, with a strip of red flannel around his neck. He must have a sore throat, for his feet are in a tub. If you want to see his legs, slit the tub and you will find them.

There is also a little man in a violet, but he is much smaller and therefore much harder to find. You can look for him, though, if you have good eyesight!

JACK-IN-THE-PULPIT

Jack-in-the-pulpit is a sturdy fellow. You will find him growing in the woods, a few feet tall, with his pulpit perched atop a thick stem. Inside the pulpit you will find Jack, dignified and straight.

If you find Jack-in-the-pulpit plants which are not on private property or in a national park, you can dig up one or two and replant them in a shady spot in your garden. There they will grow nicely for many years.

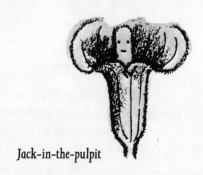

Jack-in-the-pulpit

Poppy doll

POPPY DOLL

Have you ever made a poppy doll? First, turn the petals of a full-blown poppy down over the stem. The seed pod becomes the doll's head, complete with fringed bangs, and the petals form the dress. Now snip off a bit of poppy stem and slip it through the top part of the doll's body to form the arms. Tie a sash—a blade of soft grass—around her waist and see how nicely her skirt billows out.

HOLLYHOCK LADIES

Do you have a border of hollyhocks along your back fence? If not, be sure to plant some, so that next year you will be able to make dozens of hollyhock ladies.

Here is how to make them:

First pick an equal number of hollyhock flowers and hollyhock buds. You will need some bits of twig, too, and a shallow pan of water.

Turn a blossom upside-down. It will be the doll's body. At the top, skewer a hollyhock bud to the stem with a bit of twig to form the doll's head. Insert a longer twig crosswise through the calyx, just below the head, to make the arms. Now you have a lady in a lovely frilly gown, all ready for a party.

Float the ladies in the pan of water. Blow them gently and see them dance and turn in a stately minuet!

If you would like hats for the ladies, just look around your garden. Any bell-shaped flower will be just right for a bonnet. You can put Canterbury bells on some of the ladies, while others may wear cosmos, petunia or nasturtium hats. You can even pin a rose petal to a hollyhock lady's head. If the day is very sunny, give your ladies each a nasturtium-leaf parasol with a straight twig for a handle.

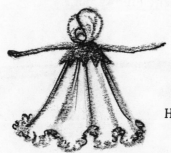

Hollyhock doll

Cut off end of petals,
paint a face

Tie two long petals
in a bow

GRANDMOTHER DAISY

To make a grandmother with a frilly nightcap, ink a face on the yellow part of the daisy. Use scissors to clip off half of all the petals but two at the bottom of the face. The two uncut petals are ribbons to tie under "grandmother's" chin.

Milkweed pod boat

MILKWEED BOATS

When you go for a ride or a walk in the country, keep your eyes open for milkweed growing along the road. Go back in the late summer or early autumn when the pods have burst open, and pick some. After you clean out the fluff, the pods will keep almost indefinitely.

You will find many uses for these seed pods. They will make boats and cradles for your flower dolls. If you have saved the downy seeds, you can stuff tiny pillows for your dolls.

Milkweed boat
as place card

A bird bath makes a perfect pond on which to sail your milkweed boats, but a pan of water will do as well. If you use the bird bath, be sure to take the boats out of the water when you are through playing. The birds may not like boats sailing around in their tub!

Milkweed pods make attractive nut cups for a party. Spray them silver or gold inside and spray the fuzzy outsides red or green. For an autumn party you can leave the pods their natural color, for the insides are a lovely golden tan.

To use the pods for table decorations, fill them with bits of evergreen and tiny flowers, either real or artificial.

To use the milkweed boats as place cards, tuck a small name card in each one, or make them into real sail boats. Write the guests' names on sail-shaped slivers of white paper and use toothpicks as masts. Put a little clay in each boat and poke in a mast.

Snapdragons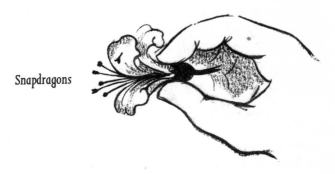

SNAPDRAGONS

Some lazy summer day when you are in the garden, you may be lucky enough to see a bee or an ant opening the jaws of a snapdragon. If you are careful, you can make the "dragon's" jaws snap, too. Without picking the flowers, gently force the jaws open and then let them snap closed.

TOAD'S TONGUE

Is there a sedum plant called "live-forever" growing in your garden? It is also called "toad's tongue," and you will soon see why.

Pick one of the thick, pulpy leaves and very gently bruise it all over. With your thumbnail snip off the stem end. Put that open end between your lips and blow into it as you would blow up a balloon. The toad's green tongue will swell up!

TOUCH-ME-NOTS

The pretty yellow and red blossoms of the four-o'clock are supposed to open at about that hour, but don't try to tell time by them! The seed pods, when they are ripe, will pop open when they are touched. Each section of the pod will curl back and the seeds will fly out. That is one of nature's many ways of sowing seeds so that more plants will come up.

The "sensitive plant" is another touch-me-not. It has a fernlike leaf made up of many small leaflets on either side of a central stem. The mimosa, too, is such a plant. Touch the leaf gently, and watch the leaflets fold up. If you keep watching, you will see them open again.

HONEYSUCKLE

Birds and bees sip nectar from flowers, and you can, too! Just bite off the end of the little tube of a honeysuckle blossom and suck the honey from it. No wonder the hummingbirds love it!

You can do the same thing with a nasturtium flower, and also with the bright red blossoms from a salvia plant.

VIOLETS

It's fun to pick big bunches of violets in the early spring, and the more often violets are picked, the better they bloom.

Do you know how to make a wish with violets? There is a little hook in the stem, just where it joins the head. Link two violets together and make a wish as you pull them apart.

COLUMBINE

Exciting surprises are hiding inside many flowers. Pull off the outer petals of a columbine and you will find doves feeding out of a dish.

"Will you be wealthy?"

DANDELIONS

Dandelions are weeds, even though their yellow flowers are bright and sunny, so no one will mind how many you pick. In fact, if you find them growing on the lawn, you should root them up completely.

When dandelion plants are young and tender, some people use their leaves for salads, or cook them as vegetable greens.

Hold a golden dandelion blossom under a friend's chin and ask, "Will you be wealthy when you grow up?" If there is a yellow glow on his chin, he will. (You can also find out if he likes butter with buttercups!)

You can make dandelion curls for yourself or your dolls. Get a glass of water and a handful of dandelions and slit the stems into several strips with your thumbnail. Drop them into the water and they will curl up into tight green ringlets.

Dandelion curls

After dandelions have gone to seed, there are even more games to play with them. Hold one in your hand and ask, "What time does my mother want me to come home?" Blow hard and then count the remaining seeds on your dandelion clock. Now you know!

Hold another white dandelion globe and ask, "How many children will I have?" Blow on the globe and then count the seeds still clinging to the stem. Better blow hard, or your house may some day be as full as the "Old Woman's" shoe!

"How many children will I have?"

CLOVER

You can play in a yard full of clover all day and never lack for things to do. Begin by hunting for four-leaf clovers for luck. If you find one, put it in your shoe and make a wish. Then say,

> "Four-leaf clover in my shoe,
> Please to make my wish come true."

Do you know how to make clover chains? Tie the stem of one flower around the head of another until your chain is as long as you wish. You can use purple clover along with the pink-and-white variety, if you have any.

Braid clover chains to make necklaces, bracelets, crowns and sashes, or tie the chains from tree to tree around the yard. You can also use clover chains to make a fairy ring on the grass. Hop into it blindfolded and make a wish.

Clover chain

Daisy crown

DAISIES

It is summer and the field is white with daisies. There are so many that you may pick all you please. Take an armful of them into the shade under the big oak tree.

With daisies you can make chains just as you do with clover. Or, since daisies have longer and stronger stems, you can braid them into a crown without first making a chain. Start braiding with three stems of unequal lengths. When you come to the end of the shortest stem, add another daisy and keep on braiding.

Name a daisy for a friend. Pluck one petal at a time, saying, "He loves me, he loves me not," until all the petals are gone.

Does he love you? If not, you can try another friend—or another daisy!

In pioneer days, many girls had to make their own jewelry. One of their favorites was a necklace made of Job's-tears. You will enjoy making a necklace out of seeds you have grown yourself. The plants are easy to grow, and after the first year they will seed themselves. Plant them where they will not be disturbed, so that they can come up each year.

The plant looks like a small corn, and the seeds, or "tears," grow in clusters where the tassel of the corn would be. Let the seeds dry on the stalks, but watch and gather the ones you need before they fall to the ground and are lost.

You can string the seeds on any strong thread. They are glossy and interesting, varying in color from nearly white to a dark gray-black. They need no further finishing. For variety, try alternating them with other beads arranged at intervals.

Job's-tears

If you have enough space to spare, try growing a pumpkin or two. It is fascinating to watch. The vines spread over a large area—one may cover 15 or 20 feet of ground—and the pumpkins themselves grow bigger and bigger, until you can hardly believe your eyes.

When you pick your pumpkin, there are several things you can do with it. Perhaps you will decide to make a Jack-O'-Lantern for Hallowe'en. If so, be sure to save the

Halloween

seeds when you scoop them out. You may want to string some for a necklace or use them for making seed pictures.

Save the largest, fattest seeds for eating. You eat them just as you eat nuts. In Arabia they call them *bizzar*. Here is how to roast them:

ROASTED PUMPKIN SEEDS

Clean away the soft fibre which holds the seeds together. Place the seeds in a shallow pan, sprinkle with salt, and set in a medium oven, about 360 °F. Stir the seeds occasionally as they roast. They are finished when the shells are perfectly dry and crisp.

Gourds

GOURDS

If you have a fence or trellis where you can let vines climb, gourds are fun to grow. Buy a package of mixed seeds and you will have gourds of many shapes, colors and sizes. After they ripen and dry, you can use them to make a variety of things, from a darning egg to a bird house.

FLOWER SANDWICHES

Rose Petal Sandwiches

12 slices of nut bread or white bread, sliced thin

cream cheese   currant or strawberry jelly

butter   fresh rose petals

Spread 6 slices of bread with butter and the other 6 with softened cream cheese. Over the cheese spread the jelly, and over the jelly arrange a layer of petals. Top each with a slice of buttered bread and cut the sandwiches into dainty rounds or fingers.

Petunia Sandwiches

Spread orange bread or banana bread with cream cheese. Edge with petunia petals, so that the petals will show when the top slices of buttered bread are added.

Marigold Open-Faced Sandwiches

(Another name for open-faced sandwiches is "canapés.")

Mix chopped hard-boiled egg with mayonnaise, salt and a bit of chopped sweet pickle and spread on slices of buttered bread. Cut into triangles and sprinkle bits of marigold petals over the tops.

Flower sandwiches

Nasturtium Sandwiches

nasturtium petals	nasturtium leaves
6 slices of white bread	6 slices of whole wheat bread
butter and mayonnaise	salt and pepper

¼ cup finely chopped chicken or tuna

¼ cup finely chopped celery

¼ cup mayonnaise

Butter the white bread and spread mayonnaise on the whole wheat bread. Mix the chicken or tuna, celery, ¼ cup of mayonnaise and 8 or 10 cut-up nasturtium leaves. Spread the mixture on the slices of whole wheat bread. Cover with nasturtium petals, letting the petals extend beyond the outer edges of the bread so that they will show in a bright ruffle when the top slices of white bread are added.

Herb Canapés

You can use buttered bread, cut in fancy shapes, or small crackers which come in fancy shapes, or both. Butter the crackers, too.

Gather a few sprigs of as many herbs as you can find in your garden, such as: chives, marjoram, basil, lemon balm, mint, fennel, anise, borage, burnet, chervil, cress, dill weed, parsley or thyme.

Now have fun making your interesting little herb canapés. Sprinkle some with chopped herbs; put tiny, whole herb leaves on others. Use only one kind of herb on each canapé.

INDEX

Petunia sandwiches, 188
Pickaback plant, 149
Pillows, scented, 105–107
Pineapple plant, 161–162
Place cards, 98
Pomander balls, 100–102, 104
Pools, 138–140
Poppy, 13, 175
Pot Marigold. *See* Marigold.
Potpourris, 107–111
Pots. *See* Containers.
Potted plants
  as gifts, 97
  caring for, 53, 88
Potting, 53, 84–85
Prayer plant, 150, 151
Preserving and storing, 71–79
Propagating, 61–65
Pruning, 88
Pumpkins, 186–187
Pumpkin seeds, 187
Punches, 125–126

Root division, 61, 62–63
Rose geranium, 29–30, 45, 47, 50, 52, 82, 84, 92, 97–98, 100, 112, 119, 130
Rose jars. *See* Potpourris.
Rosemary, 13, 14, 30, 36, 45, 46, 47, 48, 52, 54, 60, 69, 72, 81, 82, 93, 100, 112, 122, 130
Rose petals, 119, 120, 125–126
Rose petal sandwiches, 188
Rue, 30, 47, 54, 60, 131

Sachets, 103–104
Sage, 13, 14, 31, 36, 45, 47, 48, 49, 60, 61, 62–63, 67–68, 72, 73, 81, 93, 119, 123, 131
Salts, 117
Santolina, 31, 60, 90, 131
Savory, summer. *See* Summer savory.
Savory, winter. *See* Winter savory.
Scarlet runner bean, 144
Scented pillows, 105–107
Sedum. *See* Toad's tongue.
Seedlings, 38–41, 42–44
Seeds
  as gifts, 100
  culinary, 13–14
  drying, 75
  harvesting, 69–70
  propagating by, 61–62, 65
  sowing, 37–38, 40, 45
Seersucker plant, 152
Sesame, 13
Shallots, 131
Snake plant, 152
Snapdragons, 179
Soil, preparing, 36–37

Sorrel, 32, 45, 77, 112, 131
Sowing
  in flats, pots or boxes, 38–41
  outdoors, 29, 37–38
Spearmint, 13, 14, 27, 61, 91–92, 119, 122. *See also* Mint.
Spices
  pomander balls, 102
  potpourris, 110
  scented pillows, 106
  vinegars, 114
Spider plant, 148
Stem cuttings, 42, 61, 64–65
Storing and preserving, 71–79
Strawberry barrel, 140–141
Succulents, 153
Sugars, 118
Summer savory, 13, 14, 32, 68, 72, 73, 131
Sweet bags. *See* Sachets.
Sweet basil. *See* Basil.
Sweet cicely. *See* Cicely.
Sweet Marjoram. *See* Marjoram.
Sweet-potato vine, 169
Sweet Woodruff. *See* Woodruff.

Table, garden, 142
Tallies, 98
Tansy, 32–33, 97–98, 131
Tarragon, 15, 33, 36, 37, 45, 48, 53, 62, 68, 72, 77, 81, 93, 131
Teas. *See* Tisanes.
Terrariums, 157
Thyme, 13, 15, 33–34, 36, 37, 44–45, 46, 47, 49, 52, 60, 61, 62–63, 69, 72, 81, 93, 112, 118, 131
Tisanes, 120–124
Toad's tongue, 179
Touch-me-nots, 180
Transplanting, 42–45
Trellises, 143-144
Turnips, 168
Tussie-mussies, 99–100
Two-men-in-a-boat, 152

Upland cress. *See* Cress.

Vegetables, 166–171
Venus'-flytrap, 150
Vinegars, 112–115
Vines, 144–145
Violets, 180

Water gardens, 158, 159
Watering, 38, 46, 53, 86
Wax plant, 156
Weeding, 46
Winter gardens, 148–160
Winter savory, 14–15, 32, 36, 46, 49, 52, 61, 68, 131
Wisteria, 144
Woodruff, 15, 34, 47, 131
Wooly mint, 27